LOVING
AND LOSING A PET

LOVING
AND LOSING A PET

A Psychologist
and a Veterinarian
Share Their Wisdom

Michael Stern, Ph.D.
Susan Cropper, D.V.M.

JASON ARONSON INC.
Northvale, New Jersey
London

Production Editor: Elaine Lindenblatt

Interior drawings by Seth Thompson

This book was set in 11 pt. New Baskerville by Alabama Book Composition of Deatsville, Alabama and printed and bound by Integrated Book Technology of Troy, New York.

Library of Congress Cataloging-in-Publication Data

Stern, Michael, 1946–
    Loving and losing a pet : a psychologist and a veterinarian share
their wisdom / Michael Stern, Susan Cropper.
        p. cm.
    Includes bibliographical references (p. 199) and index.
    ISBN 0-7657-0116-2 (alk. paper)
    1. Pet owners—Psychology.   2. Pets—Psychological aspects.
3. Pets—Death—Psychological aspects.   4. Bereavement—
Psychological aspects.   5. Human-animal relationships.
    I. Cropper, Susan.   II. Title.
SF411.47.S74   1998
155.9′37—dc21   97-23339

Printed in the United States of America on acid-free paper. For information and catalog write to Jason Aronson Inc., 230 Livingston Street, Northvale, New Jersey 07647-1731. Or visit our website: http://www.aronson.com

Contents

Preface   ix

Acknowledgments   xiii

Introduction   xv

PART I.   PETS: A LOVE STORY
Overview

1.   The Concept of Attachment   3

*Role of attachment in human development. Attachment
throughout the life cycle. Effects of disruptions in
attachment. Pets and attachment relationships.*

2.   What Pets Are to Humans   21

*Brief history of the human–pet relationship. Conscious
and unconscious motivations for having pets.
The place of pets in our lives.*

3. Attachment, the Family, and Children   39

*How relationships are learned. Regulation of emotions.
Pets and family functioning. The family, the sick pet,
and medical expenses.*

4. The Elderly and Pets   53

*Benefits and burdens of having pets. Concerns about the
future of both owner and pet. Variations of owning pets.
Getting help. Dealing with one more loss.*

PART II.   TO HAVE, TO NURTURE, TO PROTECT
Overview

5. Acquisition Advice   71

*Criteria to consider: time, energy, space, economics, lifestyle,
temperament, motivation, age. Providing veterinary care.*

6. Life Span, Aging, and Physical Decline   89

*Dealing with the inevitable. Quality of life issues. Emotional
and financial considerations. What veterinarians can and
cannot do.*

7. Legal Issues   101

*The rights of animals. Laws, rules, and regulations.
Inadequate care and malpractice suits.*

PART III.   WHEN THE BARKING STOPS
Overview

8. Unexpected Loss   119

*Accidents and other disasters. The impact of trauma.
The sense of helplessness. Taking action.*

9. The Question of Euthanasia   135

Philosophical dilemmas. Who makes the decision and how. Personal, familial, and social conflicts. The role of the veterinarian. How it is done.

10. Grief and Bereavement   143

Social expectations and personal experience in grieving for pets. The process of bereavement. Allowing for time.

11. Children and Loss of a Pet   159

Dealing with illness and death. How the family can help.

12. Following the Loss: "I Will Never Have a Pet Again!"   173

Loyalty to the lost pet. Guilt. Accepting a change of heart. Dealing with the uniqueness of each relationship. What a new pet can and cannot do for you. New beginnings.

13. When Recovery Is Hard   181

Complicated grief. What we learn from loss. Being there as sympathetic listeners. Helping others. Support groups and other resources.

References   199

Related Readings   201

Index   205

About the Authors   211

Preface

In our separate practices we are frequently struck by the overlap of our fields and by the need to understand the human-animal bond as including both psychology and medicine. The decision to write this book arose out of the discovery that there has never been a joint effort by a psychologist and a veterinarian to address the complex relationship between pets and their owners.

We attempt to accompany people from the early deliberations about getting a pet through the actual process of acquiring one, caring for it, dealing with the inevitable crises along the way, and finally preparing for and dealing with loss and death. We view the entire relationship between people and pets as greatly influenced by who the owner is, psychologically speaking, and we know that as providers of care we have to tailor our interventions to fit the unique sensibilities of our patients.

We have devoted two chapters to specific populations, namely children and the elderly, because we believe that their relationships with pets are governed by special considerations. We have also devoted two chapters to providing a theoretical framework for understanding the human–pet bond, in the spirit of communicating an even greater appreciation of what's involved in having a pet.

In our work, in both psychology and veterinary medicine, we are constantly reminded that few good things come without a price. We regularly deal with great expectations that somehow fail to materialize or with pain that has not been anticipated. Throughout the book we try to alert current and prospective pet owners to the importance of becoming educated to the realities of pet ownership so that they will be less likely to experience disillusionment. For example, pets can get lost quite easily, yet with some simple precautions many mishaps can be averted. Or, the idea of vacationing with the family pet sounds wonderful but how about the practical implications? And what are the legal rights and obligations of a pet owner? We are fully aware that the issues each pet owner encounters are quite individual. What we know for sure is that, like any other emotional bond, the relationship with a pet is multidimensional and continuously exposes us to a wide range of feelings and reactions. Playing with a kitten brings out the playful child in us, while mourning a lost dog leaves us agonizingly sad. Adopting a pet requires a willingness to experience such extremes, and being prepared can be at least somewhat reassuring.

As a psychologist and a veterinarian we come from different professional places. Though we share a love of animals, we have somewhat different perspectives on life with pets. In conceptualizing this book we decided to capitalize on our different strengths and write independently, Michael about attachment, the family, and loss, Susan about medical care and euthanasia. Since two separate voices are readily apparent, we want to introduce ourselves individually.

> *Michael:* I come to this endeavor from a social sciences
> background. My training in theoretical and clinical

psychology alerts me to meanings of dynamics, feelings, and behaviors, and places relationships of all sorts at the center of my attention. I think less in terms of what's wrong and more in terms of how things develop the way they do, so the purpose of my work is not to fix but to understand and to clarify. In years of psychotherapeutic work I have come across innumerable references to pets in my patients' accounts of family life and I have noticed the emotional investment that so many people have in their pets. In fact, inquiring about pets has become a standard question that yields rich emotional material about family dynamics and individual states of mind. I have found that people who may be reserved when talking about themselves or family members are much looser and more self-disclosing when talking about their pets, past or present, and their pet stories can serve as fairly accurate gauges of self-image and relatedness. My aim, then, is to address the complicated human–animal bond as both a contributor to individual wellbeing and, when the bond is disrupted, a psychological stressor. I hope that this book will enhance the experience of having a pet and facilitate dealing with losing one.

Susan: My involvement with the book came about through Michael's wife, Louise, who mentioned to me that her husband was writing a book on pets and loss. My thirty-three years of practicing veterinary medicine have taught me that questions about aging, illness, and euthanasia are usually not considered early enough in the pets' lives. I was therefore intrigued by the proposal to collaborate on what I believe to be a unique effort to address the intersection of veterinary medicine and psychology. In trying to keep my patients healthy and long living and my clients knowledgeable and receptive to my advice, I have felt the need for advance awareness. Let there be informed concern before there is any sadness or worry or denial on the pet horizon, so that the pet-owning experience can be enjoyable, fulfilling, and downright fun.

We have both grown up with animals and had our shares of sweet and bitter moments. We have been moved by the wisdom, strength, and elegance of our pets and also by their affection and loyalty. We firmly believe in the responsibility with which we must approach our life with animals, and we have come to appreciate the intensity of most people's affective connection to their pets. We have learned that our love for pets is not diminished but enhanced by understanding them better and by being more fully aware of what we are doing as their owners. We have come together to write this book in an effort to share those personal and professional perspectives as an expression of gratitude for the enrichment afforded our lives by our pets. To the extent that those who already share our enthusiasm develop a greater appreciation of the bond and its meaning, our goal will have been met.

Throughout the book we illustrate our points with examples from our practices. We have been careful to conceal the identities of the individuals and families discussed, but we would like to take this opportunity to thank all those who have trusted us with their personal experiences, both joyous and painful, through stories, anecdotes, and recollections. It seems that EVERYBODY has a pet story, each special, unique, and touching. We feel privileged to have been exposed to so many of them, and hope that in sharing them we have made this book more illuminating as well as more interesting.

Acknowledgments

I will always be grateful to my mom and dad for their love and support. They encouraged me to reach for my goal of being a veterinarian when in the 1950s the world was saying "No, you'll never be able to do that—you're a GIRL." And to my clients, whose loving care of their animals has allowed me to always enjoy my chosen profession, as well as to my own wonderful pets, whose companionship and love have brightened and sustained all of my days—a very special thank you.

Susan Cropper

The nature of this book dictates that in acknowledging those who have inspired me I should start with my pets. My first dog, Pooky, was the kind of mate that every child should have. She was playful, loyal, and just as scared of winter storms as I was. Reggie and Vanessa, cats of distinction, took their time finding just the right spot in my lap. Pepper, strong willed and energetic, managed to turn my wife into a dog person. Which brings us to our current pets: Howie, the sociable guinea pig; Cody, who has completed my wife's transformation; and Singe, the cat whose early curiosity regarding the stove earned him his name.

In my home the lives of our animals are so intertwined with ours that at times when we lounge in our bedroom and one by one the dog, the cat, and our daughters join us, the differences in species appear insignificant. I do want to thank my wife, Louise, and my daughters, Karen and Tammy, for sharing the excitement of writing this book and offering ideas and directions. I also thank Justin Straus, D.V.M., for his inspiration and all those who have volunteered anecdotes and stories along the way—and of course my co-author, Susan, who embraced the project enthusiastically and who never refused any request including trimming the guinea pig's nails. The people at Jason Aronson Publishers have been generous with their time and energy, and special thanks go to Michael Moskowitz, Cindy Hyden, Elaine Lindenblatt, and Nancy D'Arrigo.

Michael Stern

Introduction

Of all the things you may possess few, if any, are likely to provide as much consistent pleasure and satisfaction as a pet. Regardless of species, breed, size, or monetary value, pets reward their owners with loyalty, affection, attachment, and a sense of well-being, often over a period of many years.

But having a pet also means being prepared to part with it someday. The reality of the relative short life span of most house pets dictates that sooner or later you will have to face the pet's decline and death. In your relationship with your pet you invest tremendous affection and caring, and the longer the relationship exists the stronger the bond becomes. Pets offer their owners almost unconditional acceptance and are indifferent to the things that complicate relations among humans. Their delight at greeting or cuddling with you serves as a welcome affirmation of love and predictability and offers a sense that all is well with the world. Your pet's sensitivity to your moods serves as a reprieve from an occasionally indifferent world, and your intimate, conflict-free relationship may come close to being the purest possible form of give and take with another living creature.

Pets do not grow up and go to college. They depend on their owners' care for their entire lives, and in fact become more dependent as time goes on. Whatever self-sufficiency they are endowed with is lost with time, and whatever new behaviors are acquired are not necessarily in the service of their survival. In the absence of judgment appropriate for urban or suburban living, pets can and do get into trouble unless protected by their owners. More pets are hurt by lack of adequate protection than by intentional abuse, often in genuinely caring but overburdened family environments. Pets require regular veterinary care and special attention when their behavior or routine is unexpectedly changing. Since they are unable to articulate pain or discomfort, early detection of problems, a crucial component of good medical care, is left to their owners. Similarly, basic safety awareness, which even young children can be expected to learn, is sometimes beyond the capacity of the pet and the owner has to compensate on a continuous basis.

Unlike children who mostly live with young to middle-aged adults, pets live with a wide range of owners. Ideally there would be some match between the needs of a pet and the owner's ability to satisfy them, so that, for example, a playful and energetic puppy would belong to a young child (with parental supervision), who would have learned basic pet care skills on a relatively low-maintenance pet such as a hamster. That way neither pet nor owner feels frustrated, overburdened, or neglected, and good chemistry can develop. Whatever the match, however, strong attachments get created and the imminent or actual loss of a pet is likely to trigger strong emotional reactions. Specific reactions to loss of a pet, the way YOU handle losing YOUR pet, depends on many factors including your age, past experiences, and the environment in which you live. For children, loss of a pet may be a first encounter with death with all its existential implications, requiring very careful and sensitive attention from caring adults.

For the elderly, dying is an all too real prospect and the death of a pet can be viewed either with stoic acceptance and recognition or with angry denial or protestation. Busy adults may find it necessary to suppress their grief in order to carry on with their other responsibilities, and individuals living alone may become overwhelmed with a sense of loneliness. There are no rules about grieving but often your place on the continuum of life dictates the issues that arise in the face of loss as well as the psychological mechanisms available to deal with them.

Loss of a pet comes in different ways, some expected and gradual, some sudden and violent. Since pets are not guaranteed the same protections as humans, many are involved in accidents, disappear, or are given away. Unexpected loss can be particularly difficult to process and can trigger strong feelings of guilt and blame, but sometimes even the most predictable and unavoidable loss involves intense conflict and soul searching.

Probably the most controversial form of pet loss involves euthanasia, a procedure that is rarely considered without emotional torment and intensive debate. There is an inherent paradox in ending a life in an effort to be humane and caring, and even when the case is clearly made for relieving the animal of its misery the weight of the decision can be heavy indeed. Different people have very different conceptions of life and death and of the role that any person should play in determining when life can end. Veterinarians are not exempt from that question and euthanasia is among the least favored undertakings for many of them, also because the death of an animal is a concrete reminder of the limits of modern medicine and the resources of their discipline. However, a discussion between you and your veterinarian about the need for euthanasia can yield a realistic medical assessment unbiased by emotion, and may turn out to provide you with a better awareness of options and welcome relief from guilt as well.

Relatives, friends, and strangers are all invested in seeing your psychological balance restored as soon as possible after you experience a loss. No one wants to see suffering and some do not quite understand its depth when the loss involves "only an animal." Death of a pet fits into the category of "disenfranchised losses," the kind for which our society does not have established rituals or customs. Individuals have personal notions of what they consider normal or appropriate reactions and, in the case of pet loss, the space allowed for grieving is often rather limited. Prolonged or unusually intense grief is likely to meet with surprise, confusion, and eventually impatience and disdain. External support is often withdrawn just when it is needed most. An awareness of your own feelings as well as those of others can be extremely useful in avoiding unnecessary rifts between yourself and those around you.

Beyond the immediate reaction to loss lie the long term implications. Though people often swear immediately upon losing a pet that they will never get another one, time is in fact the healer it is presumed to be, and it often brings about a change of heart. Those who have mourned a pet and have later adopted another one are most appreciative of the bond and of its complexity, such that, rather than diluting the memory of the lost pet, having another one in fact keeps the memory alive. The decision, however, is strictly personal, and at the very least you have to allow whatever time you need to be free of guilt and thus able to see the new pet for what it is, not just as a replacement for what was lost. A new pet may bring healing to a family hurt by any traumatic loss and offer a measure of optimism and continuity. Even the younger members of a family affected by loss can emerge from the experience more sensitive and attuned to the pain of others. Those who turn loss into strength are the ones to whom people in crisis turn for support.

Much of the adjustment to the loss of a pet occurs through personal or familial efforts to comprehend and to accept. Humans are resilient creatures. There are, however, times when available coping mechanisms cannot handle the burden and the loss may be experienced as too great to permit the resumption of daily routines. Some bereaved individuals describe themselves as going through the motions but feeling detached from events around them. If you feel this way over an extended period of time, some therapeutic intervention may be appropriate, usually on a short-term basis.

Having a pet is by all accounts a highly rewarding endeavor, but it comes at a price. Attachment carries the risk of later detachment, ownership requires continuous attention and care, and life inevitably ends in death. This realization need not dampen the joy of having a pet; instead, it can help us appreciate the gift that the companionship of another living creature really is. Being aware that a pet goes through its own life cycle and that we are privileged to be part of it encourages us, often from an early age, to feel part of the larger scheme of things, and at times even to be reassured by it.

PETS: A LOVE STORY

OVERVIEW

In this first section of the book we approach the meaning of having pets from both psychological and historical perspectives. We explore the concept of attachment, which lies at the heart of the human–animal bond, in some detail, articulating what most pet owners do intuitively and automatically. The purpose is to demonstrate one of our major contentions, namely, that being connected to a pet is no simple matter and that complicated psychological processes are involved even in what appears to be simply loving your pet. The historical perspective provides a backdrop against which our current understanding of this bond can be viewed. Our sensibilities toward pets are greatly influenced by contemporary social standards of fairness and responsibility and by prevailing concepts of human needs. Cultural awareness may not modify how we treat our individual pets but it offers us a fresh appreciation of how much choice we really have in this regard.

The connection with pets is powerful at any phase of life but there are two age groups for whom pets play a particularly important role. Children, in the midst of forming their social and interpersonal worlds, use relations with pets to further define the style and character of their interactions. For them a pet is never "just a pet," but rather an integral part of their inner circle. Children's ability to empathize with their pets is matched only by the animals' inclination to treat children as members of their own species. Though not always the most reliable caregivers, children are devoted protectors of their pets and guardians of their places within the family. It is no wonder, then, that any threat to the wellbeing of the animals is taken personally and triggers strong reactions. Since that threat may be the first real life crisis experienced by many children, they need patient and effective guidance to help them manage. Children present us with so many challenges that we first address their attachment to pets (in Chapter 3), and later their struggle with loss (in Chapter 11).

At the other end of the life span are the elderly, whose relations with pets warrant special attention. Here is a group of individuals whose social network tends to be on the decline and for whom pets may serve a stabilizing purpose. Elderly individuals often treat their pets as substitute children, lavishing on them deeply felt love and dedication. The elderly are particularly vulnerable to identifying with pets' physical decline, and their reactions to pet loss can be quite severe. Chapter 4 focuses on this unique relationship and offers some ways to enhance the experience for both the elderly and their pets.

1

The Concept of Attachment

It's all joy when the new puppy or kitten is brought home, and that's the way it should be. After all, the playfulness, the innocence, and *Oh those eyes* are what attracted us to them to begin with and made us scoop them up and carry them away with a bounce to our steps and a song in our hearts.

When we speak of pets, we usually refer to animals who are kept for companionship, for loving and being loved by, rather than for a significant utilitarian purpose. The primary benefit obtained from pets is the experience of attachment or strong emotional connections with them. The term *attachment* deserves some clarification.

The concept of attachment is most often associated with the study of the infant–mother relationship (Bowlby 1979), but many of its findings are applicable to all intense emotional connections. Attachment is defined as a strong emotional bond to others, whose loss in case of separation leads to considerable distress. This definition already makes it clear that attachment and separation are closely intertwined and that one cannot be understood or appreciated without the other. We are all moved to tears when a love story ends in separation; we appreciate the attachment so much more after it is brought to an end, and we accept the premise that loss and heartbreak are the potential prices of knowing love. This is the premise that gives dramas from *Romeo and Juliet* to *Homeward Bound* such universal power.

The definition also highlights the centrality of attachment in our emotional lives and its importance for a sense of vitality and well being. Across the life span attachment relationships play a major part in defining our lives with others since they force us to tune in to the needs, wishes, and expectations of those who matter to us, regardless of their species. Thus, a person reacts to a dog with which he or she is bonded quite differently than to any other dog, and similarly a dog reacts to his owner differently than to a stranger. An essential feature of affectional bonding is the tendency of both participants to seek each other's company and to resist anything that might separate them, including attempts by one of the partners to move away. (Just think of the hurt look on your dog's face when you are about to leave him home alone.) In humans (and some say in animals as well), affectional bonds are associated with powerful feelings of love, longing, and security when the bonds are maintained, and grief, loss, and anxiety when they are threatened or disrupted. Even temporary unwanted separation causes distress (as when the pet is left with others during family vacations and both pet and family members feel lousy about it).

Early psychological theories attributed affectional bonds to biological factors, and thus assumed that a baby is attached to his or her mother because the mother provided food. Research into infant behavior as well as animal behavior has shown, however, that attachment behavior is quite independent of feeding, and is actually related to the need and search for security. A baby may play alone or with peers but will rush toward a parent when scared. Similarly, your puppy will squeeze into your lap when feeling threatened, and your grown dog will come to greet you not because he is hungry but because he craves your company. In one classical psychology study (Harlow and Harlow 1962) baby chimpanzees were separated from their mothers and presented with two wire contraptions the size and shape of adult chimpanzees. The only difference between the two structures was that one consisted of exposed wires while the other was covered with soft terry-cloth. When startled, the baby chimpanzees overwhelmingly preferred the terry cloth "mother," even though it was the bare wire "mother" who had offered food. The inescapable conclusion is that the need for attachment and security is quite powerful and stands apart from other basic needs.

In so elevating attachment needs and attachment behavior to a level of basic human (and possibly animal) need, we can better appreciate the emotional significance of any relationship in which protection, security, helpfulness, and support play a central role. For instance, we observe a young child find an interesting looking worm next to her tent during a camping trip. She puts it in a small container and collects leaves and water for it. She also checks on it every morning and probably several times during the day, she names it, assigns a gender to it, and provides elaborate descriptions of its character and behavior. What accounts for this investment? Is it simply the process of exploration and discovery? Is it imitation of parenting behavior? The child's interest in the worm may in fact include all these elements but it is also more. It reflects an inborn interest in being meaningfully connected with others and in gaining a measure of control over such connections.

We all start helpless and totally dependent on others, and we gradually and slowly move toward more balanced ways of relating. For the young child there are few opportunities for feeling in charge of a relationship, and the experience of having pets (including worms) represents an excellent step in that direction. The attachment to the worm may be brief and transient but it demonstrates the intrinsic value of such a connection. It also highlights the fact that the child actually initiates the attachment behavior, that it is an active building block for our emotional makeup and interpersonal life. Having a pet, especially at a young age, provides an opportunity to be both connected and separate and thus facilitates learning the skills required for living in a civilized and complicated society. Such skills include sensitivity, responsibility, mutual respect, and consistency, as well as others that support the ability to maintain secure relationships.

PRINCIPLES OF ATTACHMENT

The principles of attachment that apply to human relationships seem quite applicable to relationships between humans and their pets as well. The major elements of attachment relationships derive from the definition of attachment as a relatively enduring tie in which the partner is important as a unique individual, interchangeable with no other. These elements can be described as follows.

Specificity

From early infancy on we are surrounded by others who have varying degrees of impact on our lives. Only a few relations at a time are considered central, and those are the ones defined as attachment relationships. Attachment is determined not by the formal roles individuals play vis-à-vis each other (e.g., parents, friends, teachers, etc.), but by the way they are perceived in the relationship (e.g., as trustworthy, helpful, compatible, etc.). There can be a stronger attachment to a friend or to a pet than to a relative, and there are many individuals, children and adults, who swear that their pets are the only truly compatible creatures in their environment. It is particularly common for adolescents to feel that no one understands them except the dog, which is of course true. The attachment is specific to a given pet or human and cannot easily be replaced by another, which explains why after losing a pet we may find it difficult to immediately rush to get another one. Since individuals (human or animal) always differ from one another, an old attachment cannot be transferred and a new attachment, if one is to develop, requires learning the uniqueness of the new other as well as adjusting to the loss of the last one. Attachment is a significant component in many human relationships and the pivotal component in our relationships with pets.

Durability

Attachment behavior is relatively stable over time and may in fact be a lifelong commitment. It takes time to develop strong emotional ties but, once they are established, they can withstand separations, some neglect, and even minor emotional injury. We can yell at the dog or call it stupid, yet know with certainty that the basic commitment to it has not changed. The experience of attachment is so powerful that we are often able to maintain it even after the relationship itself has ended due to separation or loss. Many individuals who have had pets in their lives continue to refer to one special one in terms that suggest that the attachment to this pet is still very much alive. In some cases the attachment is so persistent that even following the demise of the animal the longing for it does not subside but gets incorporated into an outlook of yearning and even despair. Optimally, even attachments of long duration get resolved with the loss of one of the participants, making room for new meaningful relationships, but it is quite common to find individuals who lead normal lives and yet maintain a special place in their hearts for one lost relationship, usually one of considerable duration.

Emotional Connection and Range

The establishment, maintenance, and loss of attachments involve powerful emotions at the center of one's emotional life. People, especially children, in caring for their pets practice the kind of affective behaviors that are required for all attachment relationships. Since relations with animals are somewhat less demanding than relations with humans, many individuals find it easier to be emotionally available and expressive with pets. Once they get used to emotional expressiveness toward pets, they may be willing to take some emotional chances with people. Having a pet thus has the potential of improving relations with fellow humans and assisting in creating new attachments. This in fact is one of the conceptual foundations of pet-assisted psychotherapy, which is used primarily with individuals who for one reason or another are inhibited in their contacts with other human beings. It is extremely touching to observe youngsters who appear totally detached from the world around them display affection and caring toward their pets. While strong emotions may be expressed in all sorts of situations (anger at a stranger, disgust at watching the news, etc.), it is attachment relationships that provide the opportunities to experience and enjoy the kind of emotions that make us feel alive and fulfilled.

An interesting aspect of attachment relations with pets is their ability to provide equal opportunities for emotional expression to both males and females. Boys and male adolescents who in our society may feel inhibited from manifesting physical and emotional affection to other people are given permission to cuddle with pets as much as girls do. Certain nurturing behaviors that girls can exercise in doll play or toward each other become available to boys only in dealing with pets. In a study of institutionalized boys (Robin et al. 1984) 90 percent indicated that they had a special pet whom they liked very much. They turned to their pets for solace, talked to them more than non-delinquent boys, and reported feeling that no one else listened as well as their pets. The value of attachment in this regard inheres in its provision for consistent and continuous engagement of a full range of emotions (in this case allowing nurturance and tenderness to exist next to toughness and aggression).

Attachment relationships often include an emotional state characterized by what appears to be temporary uninterest. Pet and owner may pass each other in the hallway without as much as looking at each other (just as mates or children and parents can do). It is one of the hallmarks of longstanding close and intimate relations that simply existing in the presence of the other is easy and legitimate, reflecting an emotional balance between two individuals in which quite a bit is understood and accepted without having to be explained or justified. The way in which pets and people, particularly children, appear to understand and accept each other despite the lack of much verbal communication gives their relationship its sense of true intimacy.

Early Establishment

In general, attachments created early in life tend to be more powerful and more lasting than later attachments. In early childhood the attachments to caregivers are the source of virtually all security and nurturance experiences and they therefore set the stage for all later relationships. Our attachment to a pet, especially at a relatively young age, is both a product of our experience with caregivers and a model for future relations with both animals and humans. When a child grows up in a home in which caring and respect toward people as well as pets are emphasized, the child learns the give and take involved and is ready to apply these principles throughout life. The failure to establish successful early attachment relationships can have a negative effect on all future interactions. There are times when a close relationship with a pet is enough to compensate for impaired nurturing from inadequate or distant caregivers. This is not to say that pets can make up for poor parenting but to suggest that any emotional attachment is valuable in shoring up a child's emotional life. Many children have emerged from daunting childhoods to become functional adults testifying to the comfort they have found in their attachments to their pets. Even children who grow up in warm and supportive environments rarely neglect to recall with gratitude what they got from their pets, which is of particular importance in today's world in which the emotional provisions in busy, two-career families tend to be in somewhat shorter supply.

Loss of an attachment figure in childhood can have a significant effect on the ability to trust in the future. In fact, individuals who either are deprived of adequate attachment relationships or experience overwhelming losses in their formative years often have difficulties in establishing secure relationships with their own children. Once again, the availability of a pet can mitigate to some extent the deficiency in human attachment opportunities and neutralize the potential damage.

Though we may acquire pets as adults, our relationships with them are likely to be governed by needs that originate in childhood. Our conviction that the relationship with the pet is unconditional and secure addresses our desire to preserve the kind of basic trust that we hopefully originally experienced with our parents and caregivers. As individuals we yearn to trust and feel secure in the presence of others, and even those who are suspicious of people sometimes find such reassurance in their pets. Pets have the wonderful ability to be needy to some extent but to adapt quite well to the limits of emotional giving within which their owners live. In their own nonverbal way, pets often manage to coax their owners into increased giving, flexibility, and expressiveness. In fact, pets have been used to assist children as well as adults in confronting the difficulties they experience in developing trusting interpersonal relationships. Such individuals take significant risks in allowing themselves the experience of attachment and they may find the risks of attaching to pets somewhat less frightening.

ATTACHMENT: A HUMAN NEED

It is clear by now that attachments are critically important in our development as functional human beings. Though we are usually satisfied with merely saying that attachments feel good or add something to our lives, it can be useful to enumerate some of the specific ways in which they make a difference.

Sense of Security

One of the most basic human needs is to feel secure in one's surroundings, and attachments are among the best tools for satisfying this need. As a result, one of the hardest things to deal with following the loss of an attachment relationship is the sense of being unprotected, alone, and insecure. One can be flanked by friends and well-wishers and still feel incredibly vulnerable. ("I know that my children care for me, but since Whiskers died I don't quite see the point anymore," says an 80-year-old woman in a nursing home.) Attachments serve as lifelines in the enormous world around us, and their loss is experienced as a severe threat to our psychological well-being. Attachments favorably affect family and social ties and enable us to deal with unrelated trauma by providing a secure base and frame of reference. When they are disrupted, restlessness, anxiety, and protestation serve as indications of the loss of security.

Companionship

Humans are social animals and it is no wonder that our most popular pets are prized for their own social skills. The strong human–pet connection suggests that the need for companionship transcends species boundaries, and that creatures different in so many ways can benefit tremendously from each other's company. Coming home to a pet that is delighted to see you is not the same as returning to an empty house. People find themselves at times separated from existing attachments and they quickly seek to fill the void with temporary attachments. Soldiers stationed on foreign soil are acutely aware of missing their loved ones and quite often seek to hold on to the experience of attachment by such basically human acts as adopting a stray dog. Though at any given moment one of the participants in an attachment relationship may wish to be involved more than the other, the need for proximity or companionship is clearly common to both participants, especially under conditions of heightened emotional intensity, such as stress, excitement, or sadness. (Notice your dog joining in when you jump with joy or when you are tearful with sorrow.)

Sense of Being Needed

When the cat leads you to his dish and gives you that starving look he is exercising in a very concrete way one of the elements of attachment, namely the ability and willingness to need someone else. In so doing the cat provides you with the complementary element, namely the ability and willingness to be needed. Just as the helplessness of an infant invites nurturing by the parent, so does the circumstantial helplessness of the pet trigger protective inclinations in its owner. (Those who react to animals with abuse or sadistic behavior are deficient in their ability to be reached on an emotional or empathic level and are likely to have serious problems in their ability to form any attachment relations at all.) A highly rewarding experience in attachment relations is the give and take of emotional and concrete nurturance. We use such relations to both offer and receive support, and we recognize the intermittent need for such nurturance as normal. Attachments also provide a context for the expression of the basic human need to be physically touched, hugged, and embraced, an experience of which many lonely individuals are deprived. Pets are huggable or at least touchable (with the possible exception of fish), and often take the initiative in seeking bodily contact. It is this contact with skin, fur, wool, or feather that contributes to making certain relationships special and unique.

Sense of Worth and Competence

Taking care of another living thing is not a skill we are born with. It is learned and practiced throughout life in various ways including play with dolls, peers, family members, and pets. People refer to us as good friends when we prove our capacity to tune in and respond to their needs, and we are likely to be rewarded with similar understanding in return. The empathic skill is often learned in relationships with pets who are by definition noverbal, and who train us in their own special way to become attuned to their needs. From paying attention or "listening" to them, we derive an ability to comprehend that transcends the limits of verbal communication and we develop a strong sense of competence. Another thing we learn from close association with pets is resilience, the realization that we can tolerate quite a bit, and come up with creative solutions in a wide range of situations. When a child observes how a cat manages to figure out a way to get down a tree it appears to be stuck in, he witnesses creative problem solving, determination, patience, and courage. The lessons will be applied in problem situations the child encounters in the future.

Reliable Partnership

Attachments are our most effective weapon against a feeling of being alone in the world. From the moment we become aware of our individuality and of our being separate from everything else around us, we try to find reliable alliances to ease that very basic existential anxiety of aloneness. From infancy forward, we hold on to our mothers' bodies, to security blankets, to close friends, to business partners, to mates, and to helpers. And from infancy to old age, pets may enter the scene, providing further assurances that we are not alone. (Elizabeth Taylor who by her own admission has failed to secure a reliable partnership through seven marriages and countless romances is rarely seen without the little dog whom she publicly describes as "my life.") When a live pet is not available, we may even find solace in a teddy bear or other stuffed animal in which we place some emotional investment. Unlike a stuffed animal, however, a live pet has the ability to prove its own interest in the alliance by greeting you vociferously, initiating play, defending you when you are in trouble, or simply appearing content in your presence.

Attachment relationships provide a secure base for further exploration of the world. It is so much easier to go on an adventure in the company of a trusted companion than to do it alone, and even a walk in the woods feels more meaningful when you are accompanied by your dog. It is the mere presence of the other rather than a specific act or contribution that provides the assurances, and sharing an experience in silence or with minimal active interaction in no way detracts from the sense of togetherness. It is a marker of an attachment relationship that it does not demand constant proof of one's interest or loyalty; a reciprocal state of relaxation is all that is required.

Source of Learning

Attachment relationships are by definition complicated and enduring systems of organizing experience and creating meaning from it. Learning to manage these relationships is therefore learning to understand social order and interpersonal relations, learning different perspectives on life and strategies by which to manage other relationships. As we grow up we learn not just from our parents and peers but from all those around us to whom we feel attached. Our pets apply different skills and strategies than we do, and we learn from them, too. Some of that learning may initially cause confusion, as in the case of a young child who tries to fly like a bird, but even in this doomed effort the child discovers options, alternatives, limits, and diversity. And of course observation of animals playing, courting, and attending to their young teaches quite a bit about the social system. Learning does not occur through language alone, and we can get some of the more fascinating and useful lessons about life and death from our pets.

Grief When an Attachment Is Threatened or Disrupted

All good things come at a price and attachments are no exception. The psychological and emotional investment that we make in such relations becomes part of who we are, and the threat of its loss therefore becomes a threat to our security. Whether we refer to our reactions to such loss as emptiness, confusion, or depression, we are expressing the sensation of being damaged or reduced by losing a viable part of ourselves. Dealing with grief will be discussed in a separate chapter, but it should be noted here that considerable grief when a relationship is disrupted is one of the indicators of an attachment. It is not uncommon for people who have just lost a pet to state that they had not been aware of how attached they were to the pet until it died. This tends to happen particularly with individuals who are brought up to consider relations with animals as qualitatively different from (and inferior to) those with humans, and who are surprised (though not necessarily disturbed) by their emotional reactions to the loss of pets.

*   *   *

Attachments are necessary building blocks to our ability to function as individuals among others. The need and the search for the experience of attachment accompany us throughout life, and we often turn to pets to supplement human relationships. All attachments, including those with pets, have the potential to enrich the lives of both participants.

2

What Pets Are to Humans

HISTORICAL BACKGROUND

Man has enjoyed companion animals from time immemorial, not only as helpers and protectors but also as friends and as vehicles for self-expression. The domestication of wild animals (which in the case of dogs goes back at least 12,000 years as compared to 4,000 years for cats) has provided man a measure of control over nature in the form of breeding, training, medical discoveries, and most recently, genetic manipulation. In modern times our understanding of the chain of evolution has made us aware that we are also connected to the animal world as living creatures who share the planet. In other words, our relationship with animals has developed through the ages and is more complicated than it sometimes appears. Even relations with pets are far from simple. People own animals for different reasons, and the relationships that emerge hinge on such factors as purpose of ownership, emotional needs, and common history.

The romantic view of having pets, exhibited in art, poetry, and folklore, is one of demonstrated affection and profound attachment. Whether it takes the form of rosy-cheeked children sitting on an oversized couch and petting a well-kempt Pekinese, or an aristocratic-looking man gazing into the distance, hunting gun in hand and elegant retriever awaiting his command, the senti-

ment is one of shared presence and a deep bond. Such portrayals
are idealized depictions of relationships that are considerably
more complex in reality. Are the children feeling connected to
the dog at this moment? What did it take to make the retriever
such an obedient partner? Nothing in the pictures conveys even
the slightest ambivalence or the existence of any negative feelings. Human–pet relationships are typically depicted as totally
innocent, even though the story of the evolution of pets as human
playmates is far from innocent. Each of us may indeed love his or
her pet in a profound way, but love in no way precludes the
surfacing of anger, resentment, aggression, and other politically
incorrect feelings at certain times.

Historical documents about families and social structures as
recent as the middle ages are remarkably silent regarding the
affectional relationships between people and their animals as
compared with their practical use. English court records, for
example, chronicle disputes involving cats (Manhawalt 1986), but
it appears that the complaints were about losing a good mouse
catcher rather than a companion. And speaking of cats, attitudes
toward them have shifted dramatically through history. They were
considered gods in ancient Egypt, demonized in the middle ages,
only to be welcomed again when rats swept through Europe and
cats' skills at catching them proved extremely useful. In the
United States cats had a less turbulent history, but then they made
their first appearance on our shores only as late as the early
seventeenth century, when they served as rat catchers on visiting
ships and some probably went ashore exploring. In order to
appreciate the complexity of each and every pet–owner relationship, the story of how animals became tamed and domesticated
should serve as a backdrop to our overall understanding. A
thorough and fascinating development of this story is offered by
Tuan (1984).

Probably the most troublesome element in the pet–human
relationship is the power and domination component. Power, a
term of reverence when applied to nature, art, machinery, or

oneself, is also a source of unease, embarrassment, and guilt. The exercise of power involves destruction and devouring, and the history of mankind reveals an unending quest for power over the environment. Man's power over trees has created cut wood and potted plants, power over animals has assured a steady supply of meat, pets, and work animals, and power over fellow humans established slavery as a social institution. Every culture has had to contend with such developments, including western civilization, which abolished slavery and has fought animal abuse (at least in terms of ending animal sacrifice and mandating humane treatment in zoos), and is only now starting to address the abuse of power over nature at large.

The story of man's power over animals starts with the original view of animals as powerful in their own right. Throughout history animals have been invested with mythical powers, and it was the desire to honor particular animals that led ancient astronomers to name star clusters in the zodiac terminology. (*Zodiac* literally means circle of animals.) Early science actually viewed star clusters as live giant heavenly animals. In today's culture certain animals, especially those with whom people have relatively little direct contact, are still associated with the concept of raw power and the readiness to use it. Automobiles are named Falcon, Mustang, Viper, or Ram (never lamb or puppy), and human aggressive tendencies are spoken of as being beastly. By means of control over animals, especially the wild and naturally aggressive ones, man has sustained his own power and influence. Rulers throughout history have taken great pride in having lions or falcons appear subdued in front of them, even if the animals had to be detoothed or declawed to achieve that effect. When resources were scarce and live wild animals could not be obtained, stone statues of roaring lions were substituted, offering at least the illusion of mastery over the wild. The animals were used as symbols of ferocity and as objects of art rather than as truly wild creatures, reflections on their masters rather than independent expressions of nature's riches.

Man has evolved as an omnivorous hunter, fully capable of killing prey and eating flesh. Cruelty to other animals is deeply embedded in human nature, and it is plainly evident in primitive societies where customs and rituals often involve considerable suffering by sacrificed animals, and in our own society where animals may be genuinely liked but are nevertheless slaughtered for food. The very word *game* suggests the duality of amusement and killing, the levity with which the intentional destruction of an animal is regarded. Nowhere is this duality exhibited more blatantly than in the bullfight arenas where human courage is celebrated at the expense of the animal's life.

Another form of absolute yet recreational control over animals' lives is found in breeding designed to create aesthetically pleasing objects. The goldfish was such an object for centuries in Oriental societies, where many households maintained goldfish, often grotesquely deformed, as pets. Clearly domestication is intertwined with domination—control of animals' living conditions and much of their behavior and breeding. Breeding for the purpose of domestication has focused on size, milk or meat production, appearance, and ferocity, among other qualities. Spaniels were bred to have long, floppy ears to give the impression of submissiveness whereas police dogs were bred to have erect ears at least in part to avoid even the impression of submission. Dogs overall have traditionally been good candidates for selective breeding since they offer a wide range of uses for humans. Originally they probably proved particularly useful in hunting, which endeared them greatly to their masters who depended on hunting for survival. Almost all small dog breeds that we know nowadays as pets were originally bred for hunting. Terriers (from the French word terre, meaning earth) served to retrieve small animals from holes in the ground, and spaniels, which originated in another part of Europe (Spain), assisted in hunting birds. The spaniels' extraordinary loyalty and affection to their owners turned them into popular companions enjoyed for more than their practical usefulness. Poodles were originally used for hunting birds and ducks, and even the ribbon on the fancy hairdo of the contemporary urban specimen has historical roots in the visible markers that distinguished the dogs as they traveled through water or brush. The original usefulness of the smallest breeds (such as the Pekinese) is not so clear. It is possible that some were created simply for attractive appearance, intelligence, easy fit in the owner's lap, or the unique tastes of breeders. Today, breeding for specific traits has become so specialized that standards of character and temperament have been established for each breed by such organizations as the American Kennel Club. Thus a cocker spaniel is supposed to be "merry and affectionate . . . faithful and engaging," the chow "dignified, independent, discerning," the golden retriever "friendly and reliable," and so forth.

Showing off a dog in a neighborhood park is an innocent enough act, but other forms of display clearly evidence man's relentless desire to exercise power over animals. One example is the public exhibition in zoos or shows of not only the beauty and grace of the animals but also their wild origin and how man deals with it, either by protecting it, as an endangered species for example, or by controlling it, as in making the animal safe for contact. Zoo visitors have historically been mesmerized by the sight of large animals tearing flesh apart at close range but through the safety of bars. Uninhibited ferocity and shameless killing are characteristics that modern man has mostly turned away from under the influence of social standards, but he can nevertheless remain in touch with them by watching "inferior" animals demonstrate and perform for him. The fascination is particularly strong in relation to monkeys, with whom man can identify while at the same time feel securely superior to. Bears, similarly, are a major attraction in zoos, probably because of their erect posture which makes them appear more human-like. Behaviors that are markedly different from ours are far less appealing to us and usually elicit detached curiosity rather than impassioned fascination. Children in particular look for the appearance in animals of qualities closer to their own such as being cute or playful or subservient. A child's experience of power in getting an animal to obey or to beg for food is modified somewhat in later life but remains a source of gratification even for adults.

Breeding animals for arbitrary criteria of beauty and appeal often interferes with the animal's original vigor and intelligence. In many homes a bit less vigor is not viewed as a problem, since the pet is expected to adapt to the physical lifestyle of its owner. In fact, one of the first things a well-trained dog has to learn is to sit or lie down and stay in that position at least for a while. For an active dog, however, such behavior is not natural, and what is played out is an exercise in control and submission for the owner's pleasure and sense of power (as well as manageability). Good training requires the demonstration of unchallengeable authority, and, unless precautions are taken, that can entail manifestations of cruelty.

Pets, especially dogs, display the primitive, unsocialized behaviors unavailable to man in modern society. Dogs eat without regard for dietary restrictions, they defecate in public, and they show complete disregard for their own pedigrees no matter how much they mean to their owners. It appears that in their undiscriminating sexual interest in other members of their species, dogs try to erase the pedigree distinctions that their owners have worked so hard to create. Their sexual appetites are revealed without inhibition, and they seem oblivious to being watched during intercourse. Children who are often discouraged from exploring their own sexuality are allowed to watch dogs lick their genitals or intimately sniff each other. Pets are even used to satisfy their owners' exhibitionistic tendencies as when a dog is invited to witness human lovemaking. Animal behavior may grant an owner contact with primitive and repressed impulses in a comical, nonthreatening manner without his having to violate social norms or taboos. Dogs or other animals trained to act aggressively offer their owners outlets for aggression that they cannot manifest in their own behavior. Conversely, some pet owners express their feminine or coquettish traits by dolling their pets up with pink ribbons or fancy hairdos, or by giving them cute names. Various breeds lend themselves to projections of particular character traits: poodles, for example, are often given the cosmetic treatment, while German shepherds serve to express aggression (even though poodles are not by nature any friendlier than shepherds).

The affection shown by most pet owners to their animals rests against a historical background of manipulation, domination, and abuse of animals. That throughout history most individuals have loved their pets and treated them fairly is a given. But it is also true that pets were often seen as objects that existed for specific uses and could be discarded or demolished at one's pleasure. Even today pets who are treated kindly and conscientiously throughout their entire lives are in the minority; many end up abandoned, sent to shelters, or otherwise destroyed.

To truly appreciate the complexity of the human–pet relationship it is important to acknowledge that gentle love is a choice that has to be renewed almost every day. The relationship is rife with opportunities for neglect and mistreatment that are not always easy to resist. It is only the awareness of all available choices that enables one to appreciate what a good relationship is all about.

THE PLACE OF PETS IN OUR LIVES

By far, the most frequently cited reasons for owning a pet are companionship and attachment. Man is a social animal who enjoys the exchange of love and affection and who has found in pets the ideal partners for such an exchange. The human–animal connection has been studied by both veterinarians and psychologists, but neither discipline has come up with an explanation of that connection that adequately accounts for its richness and intensity. We do know that veterinarians regularly deal with pet owners who are exceedingly invested in their pets' lives, and that psychologists routinely listen to patients who like and appreciate their pets more than they do many of their relatives. But what governs relations among people or relations among animals is not identical to what governs relations between people and animals, since in such relations a linguistic and social gap has to be bridged. Cats, for example, meow at people, not at other cats. What does this tell us about their perception of humans? Our pets love us but do they love us the way they love members of their own species? We love our pets but do we ever forget that they are animals? Though we may display affection and love to our pets as we do to close humans (down to whispering sweet nothings in their ears), we rarely lose sight of the major differences between us.

So what are pets to humans? Why do we pay for their equipment, supplies, and veterinary care, go out at night looking for them, or take them for a walk in a blizzard? Let us look at some possible answers to such questions and consider their impact on the relationship. (For a fuller discussion of the following points, see Stern 1996.)

Centrality of Pet in Owner's Life

Companionship is a major element in just about all human–pet relationships. When a pet is the only living thing in a person's life, a strong dependency can easily develop. Even when other people are in the picture, his relationship to his pet may be his only conflict-free attachment; the person then is likely to split the world into good pet and cruel everything else. Almost every neighborhood has such an individual, who stays away from neighbors, is uninvolved in civic affairs, refuses to buy Girl Scout cookies, and is rarely seen without his or her dog or five cats. Needless to say, this kind of person is highly invested in his pets and can be severely affected by their demise. While the example demonstrates an exaggerated attachment, we can all relate to the growing bonds that develop with pets over time.

Shared Experience

Major life events are sometimes recalled in relation to those who shared them, including pets. Adults often date events in their childhood by recalling which pets existed at the time. A pet's presence during a move to a new dwelling serves not only to facilitate the adjustment but also to enhance the attachment to the pet. Similarly, going through any kind of trauma together serves to cement the bond, as in managing to reach safety together after getting lost in the woods, or surviving a car crash. Mr. C., a man in his sixties, is aware of his intense attachment to his dog following the death of his wife. For long and difficult months during his wife's illness the dog was the only steady companion to Mr. C., who now views the dog as a fellow survivor of that trauma. When he says, "The dog and I have been through so much," he is acknowledging the contribution that the dog's presence has made to his struggle to survive emotionally. One can rest assured that when this dog is in need Mr. C. will be there to help, though probably at a high emotional cost.

Significant Exchanges

There are certain activities or exchanges that are unique to two particular participants such as a man and his hunting dog or a girl and her guinea pig. The benefits from such exchanges include recognition of qualities that belong exclusively to that particular partner. Just as we have a special way of interacting with a particular uncle or associate a certain way of kidding around with

Aunt Sarah, so we associate some pets with special moments that we experienced with them. The way Howie the guinea pig expressed her affection (yes, she's a female; it's a long story) via a combination of sounds and nibbles is forever associated with Howie and with no other guinea pig. The games Bill played with Blondie, his retriever, are similarly unique to their relationship. Such exchanges cannot be planned or predicted. They develop spontaneously, sometimes unexpectedly, and create the basis for a strong emotional bond.

Family Dynamics

Paws, the cat, may officially belong to Susan, the younger child in the family. Therefore, a special relationship may exist between the two, but it is likely to be influenced by how Susan sees herself in the context of the family at any given moment. If Paws was given to her so that she might learn the meaning of responsibility then her care (or neglect) of him will be affected by how responsible (or rebellious) she feels at the time. Even her anger at her father, totally unrelated to the issue of responsibility or pet care, will impact on her dealing with Paws. It is common for children or adolescents (and even adults) to vent their frustrations on the family pet. But as unjustified and unfair as such misdirections are, they do not usually cause permanent damage to the relationship and in fact may serve to strengthen the bond to the pet in the long run (just as a fight among friends often reinforces the friendship). Susan may refuse to feed Paws when she is angry at her father but she may then give him an extra snack or a hug in the afternoon, once the anger at father has subsided.

Family members often differ in how related they feel to the pet. Some consider it an integral part of the family structure while others see it as a nuisance, barely to be tolerated. When the pet gets ill, it is usually the committed ones in the family who jump into action, but not infrequently the others, the supposedly detached ones, suddenly realize how deeply they care for the pet, how much they have grown accustomed to it. Such a discovery can shake a person's role and assumptions and impact on other family dynamics. For example, Mr. B. was a committed family person who viewed life in terms of obligation and responsibility. He took care of family finances and made sure the house remained in good shape, but he rarely asked about others, avoided open expression of affection even toward his wife and children, and showed no interest in social interactions. His attitude toward the family pets, a dog and a ferret, was one of indifference at best, so everybody was surprised that it was Mr. B. who sprang into action when the dog injured himself in a fall and appeared to be in pain. The family saw Mr. B.'s animated concern and willingness to reach out emotionally as well as physically, and refused to allow him to return to his shell after the crisis was resolved.

Support of One's Good Self Image

Spending time with our pets and taking care of them are usually very satisfying experiences. The knowledge that we are voluntarily protecting those who need us serves to boost our image of ourselves as benevolent and worthy and to generally make us feel better. Even if we act aggressively and not always entirely honestly with fellow humans, we can be reassured of our decency by the way we treat our pets. We tend to feel particularly generous when we make sacrifices for them, including meeting significant medical bills, boarding or transportation expenses, and so on. We do not expect gratitude or recognition from the animals; the rewards come mostly in the form of enhanced self-respect and self-esteem for doing something without being asked to. Letting oneself feel responsible for an animal comes at a price, however, which is exacted when the animal gets sick or dies. If we are truly responsible for the pet's life, aren't we at least somewhat responsible for its death? If we allow the pet to become too great a measure of our worth, we may encounter serious identity problems when its condition deteriorates in spite of our efforts. Mr. H., a man in his sixties with grown children, was facing the rapid decline in his dog's health with increasing anxiety. In conversations with him, it became evident that the dog's deterioration triggered soul-searching that brought up his troubled history with his children. What Mr. H. had been unable to do with them, namely provide adequate emotional care and draw gratification from doing so, could finally be addressed in his psychotherapy by exploring his relationship with his dog. From realizing that his caring for the dog made a difference in the dog's life, Mr. H. was able to move toward realizing that he could make a difference in his children's lives as well. This discovery entailed considerable pain and significant anxiety as Mr. H. experienced regrets for the years of missed intimacy and started taking small steps toward developing closer ties with his children.

Projection of One's Own Qualities

It is often said that you can tell a lot about a person by his or her pet. Indeed, we tend to select animals that somehow reflect who we are or at least who we think we are or who we would like to be. Status-conscious individuals rarely choose mutts from a shelter, and owners of pit bulls tend to be on the aggressive or guarded side. (These are of course wild generalizations but, just as we judge people by their clothes, automobiles, or homes, we base certain assumptions on their pets.) Once we acquire a pet, we often project onto it qualities we like or dislike in ourselves. A child may call his puppy stupid at a moment of feeling inadequate and out of control, or an adult will call his dog a pig when the dog tries to get a bite of the rich dessert the person is consuming. When we are at peace with ourselves and those around us, we are likely to see the animal as cute and lovable. People frequently describe their pets as wanting and needing the things for which they themselves feel a need, and pets are usually willing participants in this process. They naturally adopt their owners' behavioral styles, which is precisely what makes their eventual loss so difficult to accept: we lose not only the pet but also the part of ourselves we projected onto it. Mrs. O. described her dog as totally unable to care for himself; she would lead him by the collar to his food dish. No amount of assurances by the veterinarian that the dog would in fact find his dish on his own did any good. When she was later referred for psychological counseling by her daughter, the extent of Mrs. O.'s terror of caring for herself in light of the daughter's move to another town surfaced. She did become able to function on her own and to let the dog find his way to the dish, yet she continued to describe the dog's feelings as lonely, depressed, and helpless. The dog, by now conditioned to wait for help, made similarly tentative progress toward self sufficiency.

Association of Pet with Another Person

When we inherit a pet that previously belonged to a person we know, it is not unusual to describe the pet in terms more representative of the person than of the animal itself. It is also not unusual to experience feelings toward the animal that were originally felt toward the person, such as deep affection or subtle disdain. In one extreme such case, a young woman who had had a very conflicted relationship with her mother was charged with the care of the mother's cat, much to her chagrin. She briefly considered placing the cat in a shelter or even having it euthanized, but was quickly overwhelmed by guilt and remorse over such temptations. She proceeded to provide for the cat, but in the same conflicted and ambivalent style that had characterized her relationship with her mother. When the cat became sick and died, the woman was beside herself with recriminations; only gradually and with professional help was she able to recover and to recognize some relief at finally getting away from the concrete reminder of her tortured relationship with her mother. Even in less extreme cases, the loss of a pet with which one has had an ambivalent relationship may trigger a stormy grief reaction. The death of an animal that had belonged to a relative or friend now deceased may reawaken the original sense of loss or add to it. Sometimes this secondary grief can be expressed more openly than the primary grief, which may have been muted or suppressed. Miss L., for example, was in shock and emotional withdrawal when her uncle died in a car accident with two other family members. At the time she was the only one in a position to adopt the uncle's dog, and she did so and cared for it for three years. When the dog died after a fairly short illness, she was flooded by memories of her uncle and the tragedy of his death, and her feelings of pain, anger, and despair led her to seek psychological help, from which she could and did benefit.

Affirmation of Views on Life and Death

Our attitudes toward pets are governed by our philosophical and moral assessment of the nature of life and death and of the roles that humans and animals play vis-à-vis one other. Attachment to a pet may serve to express mourning for past losses or affirmation of continuing life. Witnessing the progression of a pet's life cycle from birth to death drives home not only the wonders of life but also the inevitability of death. Pets may be seen as the embodiment of optimism and relatedness, and their deaths as limitations to both. At times, pet loss can provide an opportunity to enrich adjustment skills with perspectives not always available in the past.

Mrs. B., for instance, a woman of rigid moralistic views, considered death to be just and proper punishment for various sins. She was unyielding in her views when several of her elderly friends died, but Mrs. B. was unable to attribute the death of her cat, Tommy, a reliable and trusted companion, to sin, and thus was forced to add some flexibility to her belief system and expand its application.

3

Attachment, the Family, and Children

Every meaningful moment in human life is colored by emotion, and all emotions are first learned, developed, and practiced in the context of the family. Certainly when it comes to nurturing behavior as well as to emotional regulation, the family is the laboratory in which patterns of behaving and emotional expression are established and practiced. Among the things we learn there are the desire and the ability to care for others, including pets.

A family that chooses to have pets may do so for a variety of reasons but in any case makes a statement to its members and to others that it is willing to look beyond its minimal boundaries for company, caring, and inclusion. Elements of sharing and even of sacrificing are inevitably involved in having a pet, and even the youngest members of the family quickly learn that nurturing and addressing the needs of others across species lines are part of rich family life. The presence of the pet suggests to family members not only that the many kinds of rewards available in the world are not limited to those provided by humans, but also that in order to receive them one has to put in work, money, and emotional investment.

Pets accompany the family throughout its different phases, and pet choices are often affected by where along the sequence the family is. Young couples tend to have dogs or cats whereas most families with small children go through the hamster and guinea pig stage (sometimes in conjunction with already-owned dogs and cats). And while young couples may be quite selective in their pet choices, families with children are more open to mutts and whatever the local shelter happens to have. The love bestowed on the animals is just as genuine and heartfelt as the love for purebreds, but the perspective on the place of the pet in the larger family structure can be different. Also, once the children reach a certain age, they are the ones who have the larger input into pet choices, and for them "cute" matters more than almost any other consideration. While adults can visit a pet store or a shelter and leave without feeling compelled to make a selection, it is the rare child who will not be won over by the charms of some puppy or kitten. So it is no wonder that families with young children are animal shelters' best customers. Families usually adopt pets not just as companions but also as vehicles for teaching children about nature, about caring, and about responsibility. Rodents such as gerbils or hamsters are hardly the best companions but they are perceived by many adults to be low-maintenance pets and manageable by children. In reality, though, many children lose interest rather quickly in animals they cannot hug or cuddle and whose care consists mostly of cleaning the cage. It is the expectation in many families that the children perform pet-related chores, but more fights and arguments focus on such matters than on almost any other and the question arises as to why generation after generation of parents puts itself in that position. One possible explanation is that the parents are not interested in developing a new emotional attachment at the time that such rodents are adopted, so they settle on an animal that puts no demands on them while still satisfying their child's yearning for a pet. It is a common refrain of parents adopting pets that they will get it "as long as I don't have to take care of it." What is meant is not just that they do not want more work but also that they do not seek additional emotional attachments.

However, regardless of promises, resolutions, and warnings,

it is the almost inevitable fate of parents to end up with much of the pet care, or at least with having to police it. This is the "You wanted a pet, now I am stuck with the work!" phase of family life, in which stronger family cohesion can be established in spite of, or maybe because of, such arguments. Children often have to lobby long and hard to get the parents to agree to a pet, and the final victory is frequently experienced by all involved as proof of love and acceptance. Parents should not underestimate the significance of such decisions. The refusal to allow youngsters to have pets is a major complaint of adults describing their childhoods in psychotherapy. It is remembered as an empathic failure and as an unnecessary and profound letdown. Parents' consent to a child's bringing home a pet, even a goldfish won at a fair, is one of the easiest yet more meaningful gestures parents can make.

Since many families acquire animals at the insistence of their children, a pet is often considered to belong to the child, regardless of who does the actual caretaking. As a result the pet becomes not only an important object of attachment and affection but also the first major subject of the child's lessons in control and responsibility. Children delight in teaching the pet to obey or to perform tricks, and they apply to their pets the principles of performance, reward, and socialization they are taught by their parents. Children learn the valuable lessons that their actions toward the pet speak louder than their words (e.g, that cleaning the cage proves their love more than proclamations) and that the pet will respond more to kindness than to harshness. They learn the limits of their control but discover the depth of their own caring. For children who are the youngest in their families, the pet provides a welcome way out of being at the bottom of the pecking order, and for only children the pet can be something of a sibling substitute. For children in general, pets provide a powerful emotional connection that is qualitatively different from connections to other people, and is usually characterized by unlimited trust and almost unconditional acceptance. Levinson (1978) was among the first to document the impact of pets on personality development, and others (Davis and Juhasz 1985, Paresky 1996) have since affirmed the impact of closeness to pets on emotional and social development. Children's drawings of their families rarely omit the pets living in the house, indicating the animals' integral role as figures of strong attachment and mutual need.

Children are also creatures of habit who make pretty clear distinctions between things they know and like and things outside their world. Anyone who has observed children and pets at play can appreciate the depth of their connection and the reciprocal dependency that develops between them. Children away at summer camp report missing their pets more than their siblings (there's a surprise!), and it is not unusual to see pets greet their young owners more enthusiastically than they greet their adult owners. Children's dreams are filled with images of their pets, as are their creative stories, school reports, and art works. Some may forget their parents' birthdays but remember to bring something home for their pets. Such loyalty, intimacy, and, at times, self-sacrifice are more than nice or cute; they are significant components of the ability to sustain mature relationships and they enhance the child's sense of mastery over his or her environment.

Pets serve as a topic of conversation and as facilitators of family communication. Even during periods of heightened family tension, people tend to exchange words about the pets, and it is often this exchange that serves to break the tension and move the family back to normal interaction. Mrs. G., a woman of about 40, recalled in therapy how, in her family of origin, discussing the dog's needs and behavior was an ice-breaker used to end family crises. She remembered how comments progressed from a chilly "Did you feed the dog?" to "I guess I'll walk him" and "We've got to give him a bath this week," each remark progressively reaffirming the family's shared sense of commitment and responsibility. Somehow it always seemed easier to offer to do things for the dog than for each other and to express physical and verbal affection toward him. Mrs. G. observed that as soon as she heard her parents talk about the dog she would know that a cease-fire was being declared.

Pets are also used in families to express feelings and sentiments that are otherwise difficult or impossible to articulate. Danny, an 8-year-old boy, started to talk quite a bit about the possibility of his bird's dying. His psychologically-minded parents avoided the temptation to assure him that the bird was healthy and instead invited him to elaborate on his concern. What emerged was Danny's impression, mistaken as it turned out, that his grandmother's anxious reporting of recent doctor visits meant that she was about to die. Only when Danny was convinced that his grandma was in no imminent danger did his morbid preoccupation with the bird subside.

Pets take various positions in the family hierarchy and sometimes are part of alliances, conspiracies, and other family plots. Not only children turn to their pets when in distress; adults, too, embrace, hug, or absently pat their loyal pets when feeling hurt or particularly lonely. If a couple is having a fight, which person the dog parks himself next to takes on meanings of some importance to both combatants. An animal becomes "my dog" when he behaves properly but is reduced to being "the dog" or even "the mutt" or "the rag" when he fails to be an ally. Pets who have come with the territory, who originally belonged to one partner in a relationship, are particularly likely to be expected to demonstrate loyalty. Many individuals report that their pleasure at seeing their pets warm up to their new partners is somewhat mixed with jealousy or resentment.

Instances of sibling rivalry in which every available weapon is marshaled to prove superiority can also position pets in the middle of a battle. An older brother will express anger toward his younger sister by belittling her gerbil, by failing to give it water even when the water bottle is bone dry, or by speaking contemptuously about the pet to his friends. Or a child may view a pet belonging to an older sibling as an extension of that sibling's domination and treat it with defiance. When guests are in the house there may be a subtle competition as to whose pet will receive more attention or be considered better. And parents, unless they are careful, may be dragged into making statements of their preference about pets which will automatically be interpreted as reflecting a preference between or among the children. At times of crisis, however, pets may also be used to express profound love and loyalty among siblings. Sarah, 12 years old and in therapy for disruptive behavior that includes rather nasty treatment of her sister, would normally not be caught dead showing any affection to the sister's pet rabbit, yet every year when the sister goes to sleepaway camp Sarah treats the rabbit with considerable TLC (which is denied the moment the sister returns and fights resume). In times of severe crisis, the comfort of one's pet may be offered to a sibling as an attempt to share the experience and the pain. Siblings are generally reluctant to be too touchy-feely with each other, even in difficult times, but are sometimes willing to invent tangible expressions of connectedness through their pets. When a sibling's pet is not referred to as "that stupid thing" but rather by name or by an accurate description, it more often than not reflects a subtle but meaningful gesture toward the sibling that he or she is usually able to pick up.

Families who view pets as an integral part of family life tend to seek out and be drawn to other families who share this view, much as families with young babies are drawn to each other. The familiarity of animal presence and activity facilitates communication and a sense of well being, reducing formality and providing opportunity for physical outreach. (People who are not used to animals are often taken aback by the physical contact that some pets initiate and their owners allow or even encourage. They watch with horror as the cat climbs all over the kitchen counter or the dog makes himself comfortable on the couch.) It seems that the presence of pets suggests a humanistic philosophy which, if shared, provides a strong base for an ongoing relationship. If families have the same breed of pet the connection is almost instantaneous; indeed many animal-interest clubs are based on such a single common element, which members use as a springboard for discovering other commonalities. Pets sometimes become the family mascot, appearing on letterheads, address labels, checks, and so forth, and even help the family define itself, as in "We are cat people" or, more specifically, "We are a Yorky bunch." Such strong identifications are established that a family willing to switch types of cars, homes, and vacations over the years loyally continues to adopt the same breed of pet.

FAMILY VACATIONS

Pets play a significant role in family leisure activity and vacations whether they actually participate in them or not. First, there are the strategic questions as to what to do with the pet when the family is away for more than a few hours, who can be trusted to take care of it in the family's absence, and how expensive that care will be. But far worse are the emotional issues that arise when some family members protest leaving the pet with a stranger or in a kennel, or miss the pet so much that they want to cut the vacation short and return home. Many family outings that start with much excitement come to stressful and unhappy endings for such reasons and it isn't always the kids who turn sour first. In one family, the mother was so attached to her dog that her husband and children had to provide continuous reassurances weeks before their annual summer vacation. It got to the point that the children demanded that no mention be made of the dog while they were all away because talking about it inevitably led to tears.

Leaving pets in kennels triggers in many people strong feelings of guilt over abandonment and betrayal. We have all heard horror stories about poor conditions, neglect, and abuse in some kennels, so we consider boarding arrangements only with considerable caution. Common sense dictates that we do some work before leaving an animal in a strange and unfamiliar place, that we ask for references and credentials, and that we check the place out ourselves. What we also have to keep in mind is that for pet and owner alike no place is going to feel as comfortable as home, and there is really no way to reassure an animal that we will be back. Even when we can arrange optimal levels of comfort and familiarity owner and pet will miss each other, but temporary separations can be managed by both.

At times it is possible to leave a pet with friends or neighbors. What is achieved by doing so is provision of a home-like environment in which the pet is treated as special and usually receives extra attention. If the animal knows at least some of the humans in the household, the situation will not be entirely unfamiliar. For the pet owner, such an arrangement offers assurance that the pet is in good hands and is receiving adequate care, and the stigma of institutionalization is avoided. One should keep in mind, however, that neighbors and friends can be relied on only up to a point in terms of both frequency of hosting your pet and sensitivity to it. When you don't have a cat of your own you may simply not be attuned to the subtle changes in the cat's behavior that suggest the existence of a problem. In terms of family dynamics there is at times a pull between some members as to whose friends will get to host which pet, whose friend is likely to provide the best conditions, and whose is the closer family friend altogether. These contests can quickly escalate and create other tensions just before the family embarks on a trip. Some families living close to each other have established mutual pet-sitting arrangements, which work well as long as the families take vacations of comparable length but at different times. One problem that may arise in such arrangements over time is that one family could suspect inadequate care or become otherwise dissatisfied yet feel uncomfortable about hurting the other family or the friendship. It is essential under such circumstances to clear the air as soon as possible to ensure peace of mind when leaving a pet behind as well as to preserve the friendship.

Even taking a pet along on a vacation is not without its

problems. What is expected to be an idyllic vacation for all often turns sour as soon as the pet, nervous and frightened by the sudden change, throws up in the car. When traveling in the summer, a pet can neither stay in a hot car nor be brought into many establishments. (We have all seen the lone family member outside a diner or truck stop walking the dog while the rest of the family eats in air-conditioned comfort.) Worse is when the hotel at which reservations have been made refuses to welcome pets, and, needless to say, all other hotels within fifty miles are booked solid. The beginning of a great vacation this is not.

It is understandable that family members want to include pets on a trip, but careful thought should be given to the practical implications of such inclusion. Is the family pet a good traveler or does it have to be dragged into the car? How have past excursions with pets worked out? Will pets be welcome in the planned lodgings? Is the family going to visit museums, shops, theaters, or historical sites that prohibit pets? Clearly, a camping trip can be enhanced by long walks with a dog, but the reality is that handling most pets works best at home and taking them away entails inconvenience and also disruption.

THE FAMILY AND THE SICK PET

A still tougher test of family cohesion takes place when the family pet gets sick. Though different family members will have different feelings toward the pet, no one can escape the tension that grows in direct proportion to the severity of the pet's condition. Children may experience the most stress but they are in no way the only ones affected. Some pets have been in the family longer than the children, and they are a tie to, and a concrete expression of, a time in the family's life that no longer exists.

The illness of a pet can bring a family together just as much as it can highlight its fragility. The concern expressed toward the sick pet can easily be taken by other family members to represent concern for the family in general and sensitivity to its emotional needs; it may provide the most tangible impression of reliability and availability that the others may have of any particular family member. On the other hand, someone's indifference to a pet's illness can leave the rest of the family wondering about the person's ability and willingness to care about them. Ms. M., a woman in her late twenties, reported in therapy that the first cracks in her relationship with her boyfriend appeared when he failed to appreciate her concern for the cat she had had for over twelve years. The boyfriend was not cruel, nor did he deny the reality of the cat's deterioration, but he clearly did not recognize the depth of Ms. M.'s attachment to her pet and increasingly resented her preoccupation with it. His empathic failure created such doubts in her mind that she evaluated all subsequent interactions under its shadow. ("It was never the same afterwards.")

FAMILIES AND MEDICAL EXPENSES

Veterinary care for a sick pet can become quite costly, and disagreements as to how much to spend are bound to occur. Too often the perception exists that the more you love your pet the more you should be willing to pay, and some pet owners may feel unable to refuse expensive treatment for fear of being perceived by their families (and even by themselves) as not caring enough. Some are haunted by guilt, usually unjustified, over not having done enough for a deceased relative, and are determined not to feel neglectful ever again. Others may verbalize reservations about expensive interventions, but except in rare cases where those reservations are shared by all family members, difficult exchanges are likely to follow. For example, should the money be spent on surgery for the old pet or to replace the car that is falling apart? How old must the pet be before you forego costly treatment? And who should decide? The difficulty is that there are no right answers. What would be an obvious decision if a human member of the family needed urgent care can be a heart-wrenching choice when a pet is concerned. Complicating matters is the fact that though insurance plans for pets do exist they are rather limited and usually reduce expenses by only a relatively small amount; there is no catastrophic insurance for pets. There-fore, we sometimes have to face the realization that we do draw the line somewhere as to how much of the family's resources we are going to spend on pets. It is important for a family to act in a way that will not leave any one member feeling like the bad guy for having spoken the unspeakable: honesty and openness, even if hard to deal with, are far preferable to superficial compliance. All too often, when parents feel that a pet must go but believe that the children will not agree, they resort to sneaky ways of handling the situation, usually with disastrous consequences. Years, even decades, after such incidents people respond with anger and pain when recalling them. Mrs. K., for example, who is now in her thirties and a mother of two, never quite forgave her parents who, thirty years ago, sent her for a weekend stay with a friend, during which they placed the family dog at a shelter. When she returned home she was told that the dog had suddenly died, but the truth emerged in an offhand comment, as is often the case, some time during her adolescence, when trust and intimacy in the family did not need another challenge. And there is Mr. E., a college student who still shakes his head in disbelief when describing how evasive his entire family became when he tried to learn the real reason they put their two cats up for adoption some years ago. What could have been handled and resolved with some anger and a few fights turned into a lifelong family argument over trustworthiness and loyalty. The prevalence of similar stories in the annals of just one psychotherapy practice suggests that openness is not always a family's first choice in such situations. Yet we cannot emphasize enough the importance of being honest during family crises when, by definition, the availability and reliability of family members to each other can spell the difference between recovery and lasting damage.

The vast majority of adopted animals live in a family context. They quickly become integral to their host families and make their presence felt in a variety of ways. The full extent of their impact on the family is sometimes not felt until that presence is threatened by illness, old age, or injuries. A family that manages to handle pet-related crises by keeping communication open and by remaining supportive of its members is likely to emerge from them empowered and secure. When, however, a crisis reveals underlying problems in trust and caring, the consequences for family life can be seriously disruptive; the family would be well served by addressing such problems at once.

4

The Elderly and Pets

Mrs. D. is a delightful woman in her late sixties who, together with her husband, brought up two children, three dogs, and numerous smaller pets. For her sixtieth birthday her children gave her a medium size two-year-old dog "for company and protection." Mrs. D. quickly became attached to him, fulfilling her children's expectations, and she is always full of stories about the dog's wisdom and loyalty. Now, at almost 10 years of age, the dog is no longer as active as he used to be, and although Mrs. D. jokes that he acts more like a senior citizen than she does, she seems to be resigning herself to the likelihood that she will outlive him and be alone once again, at least for a while.

Mr. and Mrs. L. are in their early seventies and live on a fixed income. They mostly stay home because Mr. L. has never fully recovered from a stroke he suffered a couple of years ago. Mrs. L. takes care of him as best she can, but is experiencing significant health problems of her own. Until recently, they shared their home with Baby, a mixed-breed dog who was the apple of their eyes and died at the age of 12. Occurring as it did in close proximity to Mr. L.'s stroke, the death of the dog was perceived as adding insult to injury and as proof that the end was near for them as well. Mrs. L.'s physician noticed a dramatic change in her mental status and sought the intervention of local social services. Mrs. L. now talks to a visiting social worker about Baby as many people talk about children who have gone their own way. What she finds particularly difficult is the emptiness Baby left behind, the absence of anyone being happy to see her every morning.

Elderly individuals, like any other individuals, live under a wide range of financial, familial, and social circumstances. Some are in good physical shape, others are sickly; some are surrounded by caring family and friends, others are isolated and lonely. Most can relate to a past in which life was fuller of commitments and responsibilities, busier and more demanding of their time and possibly more involved with others. Many elderly people have suffered personal losses and tragedies mixed in with rewards and triumphs, and the lucky ones have emerged appreciative of and grateful for the richness of life.

In raising families, many of the elderly have cared for generations of pets and also helped their children cope when the pets died. From the relatively secure base of young adulthood and middle age, the death of a pet could be regarded as par for the course. The focus was on the children's grief, on the family's continuing functioning, on their own need to remain strong and in control. Among life's distractions, the death of a pet could be viewed with perspective and some detachment.

The process in which the children grow up and leave home is experienced by some as gradual and slow, by others as a shocking surprise. Usually there is a mixture of relief and sadness, of satisfaction with a mission accomplished and the threat of becoming obsolete. Some important relationships and connections lose their centrality at least in terms of time commitments, and new ones must be found. There is tremendous variability among the elderly in the ways in which they adapt to the increase in free time, the departure of loved ones, relocation, or advancing frailty. There is the 80-year-old grandmother who is an active member of a national rollercoaster enthusiasts club, but there is also the 60-year-old retiree who never leaves his home even though he is in good physical health. So while some older people are eager for social and interpersonal contacts, others act as though existence alone is the only remaining option.

The elderly are often reluctant to adopt a pet for fear that it would outlive them; the ASPCA in New York reports that in fact it receives about 500 animals a year that have outlived their owners.* This is a very considerate and humane argument and should be respected. At the same time it need not be taken as the absolute and final word, but rather as an expressed concern that needs to be addressed. There are ways (including legally binding contracts) to assure adequate care for a pet following one's death, and there is the counterargument that having a pet in fact contributes so much to the elderly person's well being that the risk is worth taking. Studies (Cusack and Smith 1984, Parkes 1972, Rogers et al. 1993) have repeatedly shown that pet owners recover faster and in higher proportions from serious illnesses, and that having someone to care for has in fact a curative impact. Caring for a pet has also been shown to improve self-care among the elderly and to reduce the frequency of visits to doctors (Siegel 1990). Indeed, many people who would sit in a cold room by themselves turn up the heat when told that their bird or cat thrives on it. Especially for the elderly who live on their own, pets make tremendous contributions in the following areas:

- **Affection and physical contact.** Though many elderly people are genuinely loved by family and friends, many are deprived of physical expressions of affection. Younger members of the family are not always around, and often they avoid hugging and embracing the old, who in turn may be too self-conscious to initiate physical contact. Pets are blissfully oblivious to such human standards, however, and they respond enthusiastically to all sources of affection, physical and emotional.

---

*Cited in *Anthrozoos* 1994, vol. 7, p. 273.

- **Safety and protection.** Pets provide a sense of safety by their mere presence, affirming that one is not alone. Just as a dog appears to be reassured by human company, the dog's owner is comforted by the dog lying by (or on) the bed. Some pets offer concrete protection by supplying acute hearing or vision and promptly alerting their owners to perceived danger. (While protectors are usually dogs, even cats have been reported to warn their owners of fire at night by jumping on them.)

- **Incentive to remain active.** By being unabashedly dependent on their owners for food, grooming, walking, and love on a continuous basis, pets force their owners to remain alert and active. Elderly people who would rather skip their own dinner than go out to buy it often report that they get up and dressed to purchase food for their pets. Pet ownership gives the elderly a reprieve from the all-consuming self-absorption that often characterizes people who live alone. It enables them to shift some of their physical concerns and gives them something other than their own ailments to talk about. Indeed, one study found that elderly pet owners conducted more conversations, often about pets, than did their peers who did not own pets.

- **Social benefits.** Pets are amazingly successful in drawing out the depressed, the withdrawn, and the isolated. Even though occasionally the connection between an older person and his pet comes at the expense of interpersonal contact, more often than not the person who is animated by a pet becomes increasingly available to meaningful connections with other people. Talking about the pet often becomes the medium by which such connections are made possible. Thus, many elderly individuals join dog clubs or other pet-oriented associations, which provide not only information and concrete help but also natural interpersonal bridges. Elderly dog owners may also use the regular walks to sustain a loose social network with neighbors whom they may never see otherwise. And a person sitting on a park bench with a pet is a lot more approachable than a person sitting in a room.

- **Health benefits.** There is tentative but growing evidence (Anderson et al. 1984, Beck and Katcher 1984, Cusack and Smith 1984) that owning a pet actually contributes to the health of the elderly owner. Among the benefits reported were reduced blood pressure, fewer strokes and heart attacks, and improvements in general well-being. It is possible that the real basis for such findings is the increased activity of walking the pet, shopping for it, and socializing with it, but does the reason really matter? The benefits of having a healthy, active creature in one's life seem to rub off regardless of the species involved. Even watching songbirds in an aviary was shown to reduce depression among residents of a nursing home (Holcomb et al. 1997). Such findings are expanding our understanding of the human-animal bond.

A significant percentage of elderly individuals live in adult communities or nursing homes. In the last few years there have been numerous studies on the relative advantages of having animals in such settings either as resident pets or as part of pet visitation programs (such as those currently organized by the Delta Society* on a national level). The studies repeatedly indicate that for most elderly individuals the presence of a pet, even on a temporary basis, is perceived as an enriching experience in terms of companionship and mutual expression of affection, and that the benefits go beyond the direct interactions with the pets. Residences that have adopted animals are reported to be generally happier places in which all levels of interaction are

*Delta Society can be reached at (800)869–6898, or at www.Deltasociety.org on the web.

enhanced. Even when a nursing home pet dies and the pain is intense, the loss is easier to bear because it is shared with other residents.

MANAGING PET OWNERSHIP

The positive implications of pet ownership for physical and psychological wellbeing of the elderly create an incentive to find ways to make the prospect attractive and the problems negotiable. Here are some.

Get Help When Necessary

One of the major adjustments that older people have to make is recognizing that they can no longer do all the things they used to do, at least not consistently. Those who come to terms with their new realities can enjoy life by recruiting others to help without being embarrassed by it. In the area of pet care there are chores that become very difficult to take care of long before it is necessary to give up on having a pet altogether. For example, if there is a hole in the fence through which the dog embarks on unsupervised and dangerous excursions, or if the pet store is too far to reach on foot but the pet owner no longer drives, arrangements can be made for assistance, offered either as a neighborly gesture or in exchange for pay. The issue of taking an ailing pet for medical care can be addressed by looking for a veterinarian who makes home visits or by asking someone else to drive. It may actually be easier to solicit help for a pet than for one's own medical needs. There are those who out of pride or shame find it difficult to ask for help and whose pets are at risk for suffering the consequences. Reaching out to others seems to get harder with age, and it would be an act of genuine kindness on the part of concerned neighbors to help out with pet care even in the face of some initial resistance.

Choose a Pet Whose Needs Are Manageable

In order to be able to spend one's golden years in the company of a pet, it makes sense to adopt one that is temperamentally compatible with, or at least adaptable to, the prevailing circumstantial constraints. An owner with physical limitations may rarely venture outside. Would it be wise to get a Retriever that lives to run? Cleaning after any breed of puppy requires considerable bending and scrubbing. Are those appropriate chores for arthritic joints? The idea of having a pet, especially an active and interactive one, is very appealing, especially following the loss of people or of good health, but even under the best of circumstances stamina wanes with age, and taking care of a young animal is best left to younger folks. There are pets exquisitely suited to a leisurely life style, which call for relatively low maintenance without necessarily yielding low returns. Cats, especially mature cats, require only moderate care on a daily basis, and some, in spite of the famous feline aloofness, reward caretakers with real physical affection and company. Fish are hardly cuddly, but watching them, feeding them, and tinkering with a fishtank can be highly satisfying. The key is in making a match between caretaker preferences and caretaking limitations.

Introduce the Pet to Others

Let others appreciate your attachment to your pet, and let them be in position to take over if needed. One of the most frequently cited problems of elderly people is the reduction of social and interpersonal activities. Pets can alleviate this problem to some extent, by serving not only as topics of conversation but also as springboards for mutual support. Visiting the grandchildren for a weekend might mean asking a neighbor to take over feeding the cat; inviting help without intrusion or overcommitment is a social bonus for both parties. Next time there is a need, the neighbor is already in position to cover, and, knowing the extent of the cat–owner attachment, most likely willing to do so.

Consider a Veterinarian Who Makes House Calls

Medical care for both humans and animals has become less personal as technology has taken over center stage. Complicated and expensive machinery is now part of any medical practice, resulting in the centralization of services. The benefits have been more accurate diagnoses, earlier detection of potentially danger- ous problems, and more effective treatments for life-threatening situations. However, most problems for which people or pets are brought to the doctor are not immediately life threatening and can be handled without much technological fanfare. In the old days doctors performed miracles with intuition, compassion, and whatever they carried in that black, awkward-looking leather bag. Today's version of home-visiting doctors includes a van and much more than a single bag, but the same compassion and ability to make it all better. Anyone who has a hard time getting around even when there is not a sick pet in the picture would do well to look for a veterinarian who makes home visits. How to find one? Many veterinarians are listed in the directory of the American Animal Hospital Association (800–883–6301; website: www.healthy- pet.com), which specifies home visits as an option. Most veteri- narians and clinics, as well, have listings of local home-visiting doctors. The bill will not differ significantly from the bill at an animal clinic, and the doctor will usually have privileges at a nearby hospital where s/he can perform any necessary tests or surgery.

Use a Pet to Expand Activities

Pets not only facilitate involvement with neighbors, but they also provide opportunities for expanding activities. Owners of particular breeds of animals form groups that welcome new members, and others attend pet shows, read and collect books and publications, even write about personal experiences with pets. Some veterinarians assist clients in finding or establishing support groups to deal with issues such as pet loss or pet ownership among the elderly. If mobility is a problem, there is the Internet, an absolutely perfect match for anyone who wants to communicate with others but cannot get out to go to meetings. Just type "poodle" or "Siamese" and pronto, fellow pet owners present themselves. The pet becomes the declared topic of conversation; you don't have to look your best, you don't have to stay in touch any longer than you wish, and you can simply click off whenever you have had enough. Though the initial equipment involves some expense, the actual use is very cheap and you are likely to connect with people throughout the world even in the middle of the night when sleep eludes you. As an unexpected gift, you may even move closer to bridging the generation gap with your computer-literate grandchildren.

LOSS AND THE ELDERLY

Because pets play such a significant role in the emotional attachment systems of many elderly people, pet loss may be an event with tremendous emotional impact. The more central the pet is in the person's life, the stronger the reaction to its loss is likely to be. In the absence of reliable support systems, the loss may gain in significance. Pet loss among the elderly is followed not only by grief and depression but also by increased health problems and social isolation (Goose and Barnes 1994).

Elderly people who live alone often lack the opportunity to

share their grief with others, and in the case of pet loss the veterinarian may be the only person to witness the emotional reaction. Unfortunately most veterinary practices are not geared for follow-up support and the elderly are left to find their own ways of dealing with the loss. One study (Paulus et al. 1984) found that while most veterinarians believed that pet loss was of serious consequence to the elderly, only a small minority followed up with phone calls or other contacts. The discrepancy was explained by the authors of the study as reflecting a feeling of professional unpreparedness. When training in counseling was provided to students of veterinary medicine, the result was greater levels of comfort dealing with distraught owners (Hart and Mader 1992).

One major difficulty that some elderly experience in grieving for a lost pet comes from the fact that they and many in their environment are also dealing with the loss of important people in their lives, and the tragedy of the death of an animal is expected to be seen in a supposedly proper perspective as less serious. After all, human life is regarded as more valuable than animal life, so the death of a pet must be mourned less than the death of a person, even if the pet provided more comfort and was the object of a stronger attachment than any person. Creating a big scene about a pet when others are coping with human losses is considered bad form and is not likely to trigger much sympathy. There is an expectation both among the elderly and among those who care for them that at that point in their lives death should be a familiar reality and therefore accepted more stoically. This, of course, is not always the case, and those elderly who refuse to live by convenient conventions face a somewhat puzzled response by their peers and friends.

The growing awareness of mortality that comes with age, both one's own mortality and that of others, is handled in various ways psychologically. While some people see death around every corner, others put it out of their immediate consciousness. The first group may spend much time at the doctor's office, the second may ignore fairly obvious warning signs. The same inclination may apply to the mortality of pets. It is important to encourage elderly individuals to maintain a realistic outlook and also to provide accurate information rather than shield them from bad news. Hard as it is for a younger veterinarian or family member to discuss death with the elderly, giving someone time to prepare and the opportunity to talk about the inevitable in order to integrate it into the rest of life is a gesture of friendship and intimacy.

There may be a tendency among those caring for the elderly to remove an ailing pet so that it will not be a burden. Certainly, many people on fixed incomes are in no position to withstand high expenses for veterinary care. The heartbreaking sight of a street beggar sharing a meal with his dog is just the extreme of an all too common situation in which elderly owners stretch an already tight budget to feed and to care for a pet. Because of their strong attachment, they are often willing to spend limitlessly to save the animal even when extensive care is objectively unafford-able. A caring veterinarian, capable of balancing firmness in setting limits with gentleness to avoid humiliation, can help the pet owner to consider all options. Removal of the animal by someone else, while perhaps well-intentioned, entirely disregards the attachment between owner and pet and also may send a demoralizing message to someone who already sees the pet's decline as a parallel to his or her own aging.

When a pet belonging to an elderly person dies, the grief is often about much more than the particular animal. The person may be mourning all of life's losses including loved ones, missed opportunities, youth, and health. The death of a pet is experi-enced as a last straw, the final insult to one's aliveness, a drain of whatever energy was left. This is the reason that the suffering many older people undergo is so profound, sometimes beyond recovery.

Senior citizens have to deal with many inevitable issues. Giving up pets does not have to be one of them. Research supports the value of companion animals to the physical, psychological, and social welfare of the elderly. Pets are a wonderful antidote to loneliness or melancholy, and they provide the companionship that other family members once did. As for the pets, we should all be so lucky. Pets owned by the elderly tend to be among the most pampered and cared for creatures on earth, benefiting greatly from the experience, compassion, and gentleness that many elderly have to offer. In spite of some management issues that need to be considered, pets and the elderly are a great match.

II

TO HAVE, TO NURTURE, TO PROTECT

OVERVIEW

Pet ownership begins before the wriggling mass of wagging tail and joyous puppy kisses comes home in your arms, before the stroking of the soft calico fur of the cat that purrs and leans its head against your fingers, before the kids jump up and down as you purchase the new hamster cage or birdcage or the iguana food. Responsible pet ownership begins with advance consideration of the needs of the animal, balanced with the interests and desires of the family that that animal will join.

Forethought is truly beneficial to the entire experience. There are many factors involved; contemplation regarding the tremendous variety of pet types is a good thing; and spur-of-the-moment choices can yield disastrous results. We urge you to consult with professionals in the field, who are usually happy to share their thoughts and ideas, and to consider issues of time and space and fundamental care long before purchase. (Of course, we also recognize how spontaneity, as in, "Let's just go look at the puppies, kittens, goldfish," sometimes results in acquisitions that will enrich the family tremendously.)

Just as the dynamics of human lives change with time, so do those of animal lives. Knowing the range of what to expect—what is normal, as well as what may indicate imminent problems—is vital for the caring pet-owning family. By indicating how easily some problems can be resolved when dealt with early enough, we hope to increase recognition of portents and reduce denial.

We conclude this section with a chapter on legal issues because we believe that familiarity with laws and regulations pertaining to companion animals can protect both pets and their owners from unnecessary hassles. The law is decidedly unsympathetic to ignorance as a defense, and more than a few pets have paid with their lives for their owners's neglecting to inform themselves. Use the chapter as a general reminder of what your rights and obligations as a responsible pet owner are.

5

Acquisition Advice

Making a decision to have and care for a pet can and should be a very carefully weighed decision. There are a great many factors that should be considered, and it is almost always better for these factors to be considered before the animal is actually at hand. However, in truth, it is often that an animal joins the family unexpectedly: a goldfish won at a local 4H fair, a hermit crab brought home from a sixth-grade science classroom on the day a school vacation begins, a stray kitten that wanders into a family's yard, a pet shop puppy that a family member cannot resist. Many times such unanticipated additions to the family unit bring wondrous rewards, so they will be addressed also.

The consideration and planning for pet ownership needs to take into account the resources available: time, energy, space, the economics of the entire family unit, as well as the interest, motivation, stick-to-itiveness, creativity, honesty, and maturity of everyone concerned.

TIME

Correctly assessing the amount of time required for caretaking depends on acquiring the right information. An example is the popular but erroneous assumption that goldfish need only to be fed. In fact, the bowls or aquariums that house the fish must be cleaned frequently and maintained properly. Water changing, filtering, aerating, pH-testing, chemical-testing, restocking, plant care, bubble devices, and many etceteras complicate the notion that, "Gee, Mom, having a few fish won't be any trouble!"

Since the amount of time that must be devoted to care increases with the complexity of the pet, it especially behooves the prospective owner of a dog or a cat to consider the demands of caretaking when embarking on the adoptive process. The fact that cats have surpassed dogs in popularity* as household pets at least partially reflects the realities that cats require less caretaking time and today's working families have less time to spare. The time should not be the only governing factor in pet adoption— but the consequences of overlooking it often cause emotional upheaval within the family.

ENERGY

The energy for pet care is another consideration. Does the entire family want to be involved? Will someone be willing to brush and comb the long, silky, easily-matted hair of a Persian cat? Who will throw a ball around and roughhouse with an energetic dalmatian at the end of a long working day? Who will be able to drive the Old English sheepdog to the groomer's once a month in the morning and pick him up four or five hours later? It should be mentioned here, also, that although many elderly pet owners will complain about the amount of time and effort their pets require, it is done lovingly. One of my oldest clients, Ms. G., complains how much work it is for her to care for her cat, Oscar, and her dog, Fiddles. On only one occasion did she relax and share with me how important they are to her, and how lost she would be

---

*Spring 1997 newsletter of CLAWS (Closter [NJ] Animal Welfare Society) reported that cats were being adopted about ten times as often as dogs.

without their company. Most experts strongly agree that in addition to the beneficial exercise providing for a pet affords, the responsibility of care can actually give purpose and meaning to lives left empty by loss of friends and family.

SPACE

Space constraints are also often overlooked or disregarded by family members who should know better. For example: Mr. K. wanted his family to be involved in the birthing process, so he bred their Brittany spaniel. He did not consider that she would have twelve puppies in the midst of a cold and snowy winter, which would confine them to the indoors until they were weaned and could leave their mother. They would need an area for whelping, feeding, and exercising—so much for the family room—not to mention the fact that a growing litter of pups can get into a lot of trouble in small quarters and make a monumental mess. The same applies to litters of adorable kittens, the advisability of whose arrival becomes questionable when there are five or six of them to feed and clean up after, and they are climbing and hanging on the drapes (and shredding them with their little sharp nails), and they haven't been placed or adopted by 12 weeks.

Pet owners commonly miscalculate what happens when one of a kind becomes more (or bigger). Ms. R. had a pet parakeet that turned out to be such a joy that when she was offered a parrot she accepted with great glee. Only later did she realize that the living room of her very small apartment was overwhelmed by an enormous parrot cage, and her neighbors began to complain about loud shrieking noises at all hours. And then there was Angela, a Girl Scout who wished to raise mice for her Animal Orientation badge. Angela and her family learned the smelly way that odors and hygiene for one mouse was not the same as for twenty mice.

ECONOMICS

Economics can be the least thoroughly considered factor, but it frequently becomes the most important, difficult, and heart-breaking for all. Take the case of the once-sleek, handsome, long-haired grey cat owned by Mrs. L. The cat that I had visited with and vaccinated over the years seemed to have been replaced by an entirely different one on a day when I made what I thought was a routine house call. The shiny hair and confident manner that Angus had always displayed was gone. He was thin to the point of emaciation, his haircoat was dry and brittle, his skin was flaky, and he coughed even as I handled him gently to examine him. "What happened to Angus?" I asked incredulously. "When did all this begin?"

Mrs. L. took a deep breath and started to cry. "I told my husband," she said, "but he said that Angus was just getting older. And you know we are on social security, and there's not a lot of money left over for fancy treatment . . . but if you can do any-thing . . . please do, otherwise, Angus has had a good life, and I guess we'll just have to put him to sleep."

So my quandary then became: What do they really want? Knowing that I can't make decisions for the owners but that I can offer them choices, I wished that they had called me sooner. A check of Angus' blood uncovered a thyroid problem that re-sponded well to medication, without a tremendous expense or effort on the family's part. But—and this is the unfortunate part—the effect that the thyroid abnormality had had on his heart required more expense and more medication than would have been necessary had they contacted me when they originally noticed he wasn't doing well. Angus was able to have a reasonably long and good life from that point on, which would have been longer, better, and less expensive if the owners hadn't decided to wait out the problem.

To avoid unnecessary turmoil and sadness, preparation for animal ownership must involve consideration of what costs will or can be incurred. The hermit crab bought on a moment's impulse during a seashore vacation needs to be attended to, albeit minimally, with cage space, food, and new shells in which to grow. The iguana will also require a cage and food, plus heaters and vitamin supplements. The puppy is not just the collar and leash, but bigger collars and longer, stronger leashes, and obedience courses, and sometimes rug repair, training crates, and boarding for family vacations, and health exams and vaccinations and surgical neutering, and special diets, and so on and on. Things not initially considered can generate lasting consequences for all, consequences for those in the family and, occasionally, awful consequences for the pet.

Veterinarians are all too often faced by new pet owners who angrily declare that they had no idea that vaccinations or surgery or whatever procedure would be so expensive. It is tempting to reply: "Well, you didn't know because you didn't ask." Surprised dismay about veterinary fees and other animal care expenses can easily be averted: figures are available in advance from the professionals who spend their lives in the field. The minutes that it might take to call one or two local veterinarians, or breeders, or groomers, or pet shops, or trainers, are worth spending. It is relatively easy for a groomer to advise about the frequency of bathing and trimming of a Bedlington terrier relative to that of an Old English sheepdog or a springer spaniel. A veterinary hospital secretary can address the number of vaccinations, tests, and treatments that a healthy kitten will need in its first year; and the veterinarian will be pleased to make some telephone consultation time available for pre-acquisition information.

LIFESTYLE

Few people ask. And few realize that the friends they do ask know only what has happened with their own individual animals, hardly a meaningful statistical sample. But there are experts who love sharing information. Who better to talk to about weimaraners than members of a weimaraner dog club? Who better to ask about how much care a Maltese needs than the family who have been Maltese owners for twenty years? How about someone who has raised fourteen Abyssinian litters? And does anybody doubt that the people who bought a two-foot-long African rock python must be doing something right when that same snake is now thirteen feet long?

Where can these folks be found? Ask, ask, ask. Ask local veterinarians or their hospital staffs; call the American Kennel Club; call the Goat Fanciers Association; buy *Cat Fancy* magazine; call groomers listed in the Yellow Pages; write to the American Veterinary Medical Association and request information; talk to your local Agricultural Extension agent or State Veterinarian.

People who volunteer their time in animal shelters love animals, and they have contacts. So do local pet store owners and the lady walking down the street with the adorable Pekinese. The Audubon Society is in the phone book; the specialty magazines list advocates to call, write, fax, or e-mail. And, of course, there are always people who want to talk about gerbil care or tailfeathers or Vietnamese potbellied pigs or guinea hens or guinea pigs or tortoises.

Discussions are fun and rewarding after animal acquisition; they can be particularly valuable beforehand. It is important to recognize self-serving advice and to ask for supportive documentation, however. The pet shop owner who maintains that no one who has purchased a shar-pei dog from his stock has ever had a skin problem should be willing to connect you with those customers directly. The Manx cat breeder who says that all her cats are champions and that her premises are free of feline leukemia, FIV, and pneumonitis should certainly have statistical and veterinary papers to prove her claims. Ditto the Saint Bernard breeder who maintains that there is no hip dysplasia in his dogs.

Most individual breeders are not in business for the money.

They do it avocationally, for love of the animals. But because of this abiding commitment to a particular breed, owners may find inconsequential what others might find abhorrent. An adorable Newfoundland puppy will grow up to be large and hairy, and drool enough to wet down an entire room whenever she smells food. A beautiful Persian will leave clumps of fine sticky hair on clothing and couches. The sleekest, tidiest Boxer can pass enough gas to empty a table at dinnertime, and a magnificently-plumed cockatoo will scatter seeds and birdfood all over the carpet with abandon.

ANIMAL TEMPERAMENT AND FAMILY DYNAMICS

Another avenue to be explored before acquiring a pet is the animal's temperament relative to that of the family. Honestly assessing the dynamics of the household and the personalities of the individual members will make for wise decisions. For example, my friend Karen always wanted a big black stallion. Stallions take a firm hand and knowledgeable manner, and she was neither strong enough physically nor determined enough with his training to not let the horse get the better of her. Consequently, it was a bad—and somewhat dangerous—match. Many times, quiet people unintentionally adopt boisterous or strong-willed dogs, only to be nonplused by their rambunctious behavior. The worrisome consequence of mismatched temperaments is the possibility of aggression when the animal assumes leadership. This possibility arises not only with dogs, but also with cats, horses, iguanas, and even some species of birds.

Whole family involvement matters. So often children will prevail upon parents to acquire a hamster, a baby rabbit, a ferret, even something that requires as little care as a hermit crab, and then lose interest. It behooves parents to be realistic about what children can and will want to do, and to be ready to step in when and if proper care is not being provided. Veterinarians and animal shelters witness the sadness and suffering inflicted on social animals when no one in the household that originally adopted them to "teach the children responsibility" takes over once the children's interest fades.

MOTIVATION

Motivation is a particularly tricky factor. Does the daughter who is requesting a snake for a pet really have an idea what that might entail, or has she seen a television video where someone looked cool with a snake draped over her shoulder? Is a hamster desired for its own sake or because someone else in class got one first? And, certainly, is a new pup worth care and training and all the rest of the effort or is the attraction the memory of fun with a childhood dog? On the positive side, there's the single, new college graduate in her first apartment, who knows without question that having a presence to come home to in the form of a warm furry kitty justifies the effort and expense and time involved; or the mom and dad and two grade-school kids who have thoroughly worked out who will do the walking, brushing, feeding, and training as well as playing with a new puppy; or the Cub Scout so eager to earn a merit badge in animal care that he has persuaded his parents that he can afford and care for the two young guinea pigs a classmate has for sale; or the retiree who has always looked forward to setting up a salt water tank with exotic fish from around the world.

AGE

Probably one of the most important considerations that relate to the wisdom of pet acquisition concerns age—the age of the prospective pet as well as the age(s) of the adoptive owner(s). Almost all young kittens, for instance, are sweet, loving, playful, and interested in companionship. They interact with the world around them, and they frolic and explore with abandon. However, after about six or seven months the lifetime personality of the cat begins to emerge, and, almost regardless of the environmental situation, that emerging personality is virtually unalterable. The result, often unfortunate, is that the kitten becomes an entirely different cat.

The kitten that would purr and snuggle warmly, becomes aloof and uninterested; the little ball of fluff that was always underfoot, or doing some wonderful antic, retreats and prefers solitude; the prankster who played lovingly with the old arthritic family dog now strikes out when he walks near. While these are extreme examples, they are not at all uncommon. (Frequently, these changes occur at exactly the right age for surgical neutering, and the animal's new behavior is erroneously attributed to its treatment at the veterinary hospital.) The point here is that knowledge can influence acquisition decisions. Would adoptive owners prefer to start with a 6- or 7-month-old cat whose personality is already established? Are they willing to exchange approximately eleven to thirteen years of adult behavior for the antics of kittenhood? Will they go to the expense of buying a purebred cat in order to have the best chance of anticipating its behavior by investigating the family line?

As for the age of the prospective owner, one issue involves the disposition of the animal when the primary caretaker is no longer available. The dog originally adopted for only Jimmy may become a beloved family member by the time Jimmy goes off to college. Or the cat that the children wanted, but then ignored, may become bonded to the father who took over feeding duty. However, along these lines, most veterinarians would argue *against* the thought that an older person should not adopt a pet because s/he is approaching the end of the life-span. Many clients confide that they will have to live longer, exercise more, be more vitally aware than otherwise, specifically because of their responsibilities toward their animal companions, who fill a real void in this era of fractured and far-flung family units.

Another age-related issue concerns the readiness of a child to cope with loss of an animal. The new pet that is purchased to replace one for which a youngster is grieving should be carefully considered: How close should the resemblance be? Indeed, should the breed or species be different? Hermit crabs are easy to care for, but they don't live very long. Fresh water fish generally live longer than salt water fish, but they usually die unexpectedly. Since few species of salt water fish can be bred commercially, most are captured from the oceans and arrive severely stressed at the local aquarium store.

PROVIDING VETERINARY CARE

Once acquired, a pet will need preventive and regular medical care. There are few things that animal people find as troubling as watching an animal contract an easily preventable life-threatening disease, like rabies, distemper, parvovirus, canine hepatitis, or feline leukemia. A family should be prepared to vaccinate dogs and cats, and provide regular veterinary exams for horses, ferrets, goats, and turtles, too. Finding a competent veterinary doctor with an interest in birds, gerbils, or snakes is not as hard as it used to be, but the time to look for one is not when an emergency arises but long before, even before the new pet joins the family. It is wise to pre-select the practitioners and veterinary facilities or boarding kennel that will be integral to the life of a pet. Knowing beforehand that the facility is clean, well cared for, and that the people involved act in a pleasant and interested manner is not a guarantee that the care will be perfect, but it is certainly a better idea than making an appointment to board your dog in a new place, rushing in as you are about to leave on a week's vacation to discover that the place is dirty and that the help is surly, and being

left with not much choice but to leave the pet with great mis-
givings—or skip the vacation.

There should be vigilance concerning simple things: for
example, not letting Rover become obese and potentially un-
healthy; keeping water available so that your box turtles don't
dehydrate; checking the top of the fish tank to prevent the moray
eel from climbing out; leashing a puppy in the front yard so that,
momentarily unobserved, she cannot scamper to her doom. Be
careful that the new kitten doesn't manage to slip between the
front door and the screen to spend a disastrous day locked in a
small space with little room to move. Know that if you tie the dog
up with a rope or chain, there is no way that he can get so tangled
that he can't breathe, or that she can hang herself by trying to
jump over something and getting caught half-way over. And cover
the garbage can/waste basket so that Rover or Tiger doesn't wind
up in the animal hospital to have chicken bones, pantyhose, or
plastic bags removed surgically from his intestinal tract. A dog we
know was fond of emptying the bathroom wastebasket and eating
discarded dental floss and used razor blades before luckily being
caught in the act. Now the worst he can get to is tissues or empty
toilet paper rolls.

These things are all experiences my clients have had with
their pets: things they knew better than to let happen, but with
pets, sometimes a little inattention and carelessness can result in
very unhappy circumstances. Think about what will be going on
in your pet's day—it doesn't take too long.

Make sure the food and water, vaccinations, exercise, and
grooming are what the experts you've consulted recommended,
and if you're not sure, or if the animal seems to feel differently
about what you're offering or doing, ask again.

Day-to-day caring for pets is rewarding, but it requires
prudence and vigilance, and consists of attending to minute
details and staying one step ahead of the animals. It sometimes
helps to think like a bird or a dog or a cat in order to anticipate
such likely behavior as getting out through an open window or

running across the street. It also helps to determine who is to do what with the pet so that no animal goes hungry because every person in the family assumed that somebody else was in charge of feeding.

EXOTICS

The explosion in the field of veterinary medicine described as "Exotic animals" encompasses animal ownership and enjoyment of many species that have not been traditionally thought of as family pets. There is now a tremendous amount of information available about these exotics, "pocket pets," and birds—their life cycles, life lengths, nutritional needs, reproductive habits, aging characteristics, and probable medical problems. Many veterinary practices now offer exotic animal care that was not available as little as five years ago. Veterinary research and knowledge has increased dramatically and has been eagerly embraced by the owners of pocket pets, reptiles, and birds.

Birds are among the most popular exotics. Today, birds of many species and breeds and an enormous range of colors, sizes, temperaments, habits, and life spans have become family pets. Many have playful personalities and are tame enough to handle and allow outside the cage; many develop strong individual bonds with one or more family members, play gleefully with toys, and look beautiful besides. Others, however, are short-lived, noisy, and disagreeable; some scream, pick their feathers, leave frequent, messy droppings, and as they get older acquire diseases and conditions that call for considerable treatment. Birds' life spans range from the four to five years of a finch to fifteen to fifty years of a cockatoo.

Ferrets, too, have become very popular: in 1990 it was estimated that seven million ferrets live as family pets (Quesembery and Hillyer 1994). Both male and female are usually neutered (sexually altered) before sale, or, failing that, as soon after acquisition as possible. Intact males can become quite aggressive; and intact females can remain in heat for long periods of time, which renders them subject to an estrogen-induced disorder that may result in a fatal anemia. Middle age comes to the average ferret at three to four years, and it is then that geriatric veterinary work-ups should begin.

The life span of exotic fish species vary greatly with their source, mode of capture, and history of early confinement. While some freshwater fish can live fifteen years, wild saltwater fish suffer irreparable damage in the course of their rude capture, incarceration, and removal from home territory. The methods of capture are barbaric: one involves using a slurp gun to literally suck the fish into a waterfilled chamber; another, even more horrible, involves dynamiting a whole reef (and sometimes additionally injecting cyanide or formaldehyde into the water), then collecting what little of the underwater population is only stunned and not dead for packaging and shipping to aquarium markets around the world.

These creatures are already damaged and probably doomed, so even though fish fanciers at the end points do their utmost to provide good, safe environments for their acquisitions, transplantation of exotic fish usually ends in outright failure or early death. A promising movement toward captive breeding of marine life can yield already-adapted aquarium specimens of fish, corals, clams, anemones, crabs, and aquatic invertebrates for the home enthusiast.

Once again, it is vital to bear in mind that "a small purchase at the fish store for little Stevie who wants some pretty ones" will not be welcomed back where it came from any more than the small iguana or python, or boa constrictor, or alligator, which grows up to be a BIG one, will be. Suddenly, the family owns an animal difficult to house and potentially dangerous. That likelihood should be considered prior to acquisition of creatures that zoos don't want and aquariums already have.

Many illnesses and some deaths in animals, as in people, can be entirely prevented with the use of proper vaccines, correct nutrition, and appropriate care. Others are rooted in genetic carelessness or overbreeding. Inbreeding refers to the incidental reproduction of undesirable characteristics in the process of genetically enhancing or doubling those that are desirable in form, function, or behavior.

Consider the Persian cat, the English bulldog, and every veterinarian's favorite adorable medical disaster, the shar-pei. The breedings that have produced the beautiful eyes and pushed-in faces of the Persians, and the pugged-faced, short-nosed, closed-nostril bulldog muzzles, have resulted in a host of medical problems such as skin lesions of moist eczema, excessive tearing of the eyes, and inflammation of the facial folds. The precious bundle of wrinkles that is a shar-pei outgrows the wrinkles, but not necessarily the facial changes that make routine sanitation of the ear canal almost impossible. This can lead to recurrent ear infections and/or abnormal eyelid conformation requiring surgery.

The hazard of asking a veterinarian for an opinion about a breed or species is that his or her experience may be concentrated on its characteristic medical problems. Lovers as well as healers must be consulted for a well-rounded picture, yet the importance of being prepared for the down sides cannot be emphasized too strongly.

A family is at risk of incurring anguish and expense if they purchase a German shepherd, a Newfoundland, or a rottweiler and have no awareness of canine hip dysplasia. This is a dreadful congenital condition especially prevalent among the large and giant breeds although any dog can carry it. When Ms. D. bought her first German shepherd, she had no idea what could happen with the hips, so she never knew to ask for verification that the parents of her new puppy had themselves been examined and found healthy and free of radiographic signs of potentially devastating dysplasia. Although even that would not have totally guaranteed that her beloved Margo would be free of the disease, it would certainly have maximized the chances. Ms. D.'s learning experience was traumatic for them both, but Ms. D. knew that she still loved the breed, so after Margo was gone and she chose to adopt another shepherd, she proceeded more wisely.

When Mr. N. bought a bichon frise puppy he had no idea that the luxated patella Bianca had inherited from her mother would probably require surgery sometime in her life. On the other hand, when Ms. P. went to fulfill her dream of owning a cocker spaniel, she did know that it was important that the eyes be checked for certain characteristic diseases, and when Mr. C. added a new kitten to his household, he made sure that it had already been tested and proved negative for infectious feline leukemia as well as feline AIDS. (These two contagious, life-threatening diseases can and should be ruled out before admitting any cat into the home.) An uninvestigated cat can appear deceptively normal, yet pass on a fatal condition to another; also, an affected but symptom-free cat may go from apparently healthy to terminal in a matter of days. Here also, prior knowledge can prevent tragedy: vaccination is available against one of these diseases and reliable tests exist for both.

6

Life Span, Aging, and Physical Decline

Most of our usual pets have far shorter life spans than their human families, though expectable length varies from species to species and sometimes from breed to breed. It is a good idea to ascertain expectable life spans and likely variations and take both into account in the process of making the initial acquisition decision. The usual life span of a mixed-breed terrier, for instance, is fourteen to sixteen years, but one of my dogs lived to be 23 years old: Tuffy—who always lived up to his name—came to me as a patient, and after a series of misadventures and accidents, wound up as my pet for twenty more years! Similarly, while many cats die sometime in their teens, veterinary practices are commonly seeing cats in their twenties.

These longer lifetimes can outlast the children's school years, and that pleasant surprise can cause difficulties for a pet and, correspondingly, for the family.

The Rose family adopted Bubbles, a miniature poodle puppy, when their daughter, Jeannie, was 8 years old. When Jeannie graduated from college at 23, Bubbles was still going strong. The Roses' growing desire to travel was affected by their concern that Bubbles, who didn't see or hear very well, wasn't used to being away from her home. The clash between their wishes and Bubbles' introduced resentment into their affection for her, and they recognized that they would have been wise to begin consid-

ering options for outside care when Bubbles was younger. Fortu-
nately, the Roses were able to find someone responsible to come
in to care for Bubbles so they could enjoy their new-found
freedom. However, they could have had plans in place much
earlier if they had realized that Bubbles would probably live to 15
or 16 and possibly live to be 20.

Not all families with aging animals remain as devoted as the
Roses. Sometimes an older pet is uprooted and dislocated,
shunted off to unfamiliar surroundings at a time of life when
adjustment is difficult. When the commitment to caretaking no
longer exists, a pet may well be better off elsewhere, but the
callousness demonstrated by such disregard casts doubt on the
genuineness of the affection up to that point. It is a sad fact that
many pets are euthanized or otherwise destroyed or badly treated
when they are guilty of nothing more than longevity. Mr. L. is
annoyed that Queenie has grown old and needs to go out more
often, but his kids aren't around much any more to take her out.
Well, the kids were starting high school when Queenie was a pup;
how can Mr. L. be surprised?

Prior to adopting a pet, adults should realize that family
structure changes when children move out of the home, and that
they, too, therefore, must make a commitment to the animal.

Sometimes the adults forge a new and stronger bond with
Jimmy's dog, or begin to have a closer and warmer relationship
with the cat who always slept on Sally's bed. Rusty, the Airedale,
was inseparable from Mike as he was growing up, but Mike is in
the Army now, stationed in Alaska, and Rusty helps fill an
enormous and unmentioned void in the life of his dad; indeed,
when they talk on the phone about Rusty's antics, father and son
are able to share something special.

Often, the bond also goes the other way; as in the case of
Oreo, who belonged to an elderly couple, both gone now. Now
Oreo, 16, lives with their son, Peter, and his wife and three
children, who can remember how Oreo used to chase Grandma's
knitting needles and chew on Grandpa's pipe. Or a client will

relate that her pet, like Mr. B.'s Yorkie, Mufflet, was a gift from her late husband before he passed away. They loved the dog together; Mufflet's companionship has not only helped to ease Mrs. B's pain but also to keep alive her connection to her husband.

On the other side, the shortness of animal lives can often cause great pain and terrible grief. Although the wrenching difficulty that loss of a loved one presents cannot be avoided because pets do die, knowing what to expect—for instance, that smaller breeds of dogs often live twice as long as giant breeds— may condition the decision about what breed to choose in the first place. So, when someone asks me about how long my Bernese mountain dog, Crash, will live, I reply that "on average, eight to ten years is probably the longest." This thought is hateful to me, but I am preparing myself as much as possible for what I know to be inevitable, and because I like to snuggle up to a big fuzzy dog, that is the choice I have made.

Not surprisingly, people feel cheated when pets fail to live out their predicted life spans.It is wise to find out from other pet owners, veterinarians, breeders, and knowledgeable personnel in pet shops and aquariums some of the things that can go wrong and shorten those life spans. Mr. J.'s understanding of his own prostate problems makes it easy for him to relate to those of his Husky, Bear. People are commonly astounded to discover that tartar and plaque accumulate on animals' teeth. Often my older clients are tickled by the suggestion that an electrocardiogram or a sonogram could help assess their pets's cardiac problems.

Advances in medicine have led to longer, healthier, and more active lives. Pet owners want (in fact, often demand) that veterinary medicine and techniques be as efficient and productive as human medicine. Thirty years ago, a routine ECG (electrocardiogram) for a pet would not have been recommended; twenty years ago, an endoscopic exam on a ferret would have been an impossibility, a CAT scan on a cat would have been unheard of, and an MRI on a dog was beyond any diagnostic dreams. Today they are all done fairly frequently. Pet owners are already familiar with the terminology, because they or someone they know has undergone one or more of these procedures. Thus, prior knowledge and experience can help yield a more informed decision about health care for their pets.

THE AGING PET

Many conditions relate directly or indirectly to the aging process. Some things may be inevitable for a specific animal, but others are results of improper care. For instance, Mr. and Mrs. M. thoughtlessly tied their 14-year-old collie, Rex, outside on their porch. Rex had always liked lying out on the porch, and the family has not realized that he had become so much more sedentary. Also he was occasionally incontinent with a not-too-well-cared-for coat. His inactivity allowed flies to lay their eggs on him; maggots had hatched and burrowed underneath his long hair, undiscovered, and they were actually eating through his skin.

Negligence is often unintentional. The R. family vaccinated their cat, Chloe, faithfully every year until she was 15. Then, at the time when Chloe's vaccinations were due, they discussed how much Chloe hated to ride in the car, how much they hated putting her in the carrier, and how since she'd had all her shots since she was little, they'd let it "go for a while." The consequences of such a decision can range from none to life-threatening. Chloe might continue to carry a protective titer against feline distemper or panleukopenia. Or she might not. If she has no natural or residual protection, and she breathes in airborne virus particles, she could contract a fatal disease, or at least suffer for a very long time and remain with a compromised immune system. In addition, by foregoing Chloe's annual veterinary examination, her owners lose the chance to have other problems identified. If she has, for example, a heart irregularity that could be treated with medication, if diagnosed early enough, finding it would substantially extend Chloe's quantity and quality of life. And, at that same missed visit, the practitioner might have discussed the tartar and plaque affecting Chloe's teeth and gums, causing inflammation, gingivitis, and decay. The family could have asked the veterinarian to clean, scale, and polish Chloe's teeth in order to preserve them, to avert infections and abscesses, and to eliminate the awful odors from her mouth that reduced everyone's pleasure in holding her. (Halitosis is common in older cats and dogs who suffer from undiagnosed or untreated dental disease.)

Tumors, skin problems, ear problems, and ingrown toenails are frequently missed by even the most conscientious owners. Something as simple as a report to the veterinarian that Chloe is acting fine but seems to be drinking more water than usual can alert the doctor to look for early signs of critical kidney, liver, and/or pancreas conditions. These happen to be among the most common causes of trouble in older cats and dogs; catching them early on can make a tremendous difference in the rest of the animal's life, and they can often be greatly ameliorated by nothing more difficult or expensive than a change in diet. So, Chloe's family was not doing her any favors by putting off her vaccinations and check-up. If they had made contact with the doctor, they might have been apprised of some options, such as tranquilizing Chloe before her visit or acclimating her to her carrier in advance; the veterinarian might have suggested ideas to make the entire visit easier, or even revealed that s/he had initiated a house call service or become associated with someone else who had.

Improper care can be much more subtle than something as blatant as tying Fido outside all day in inclement weather or with inadequate shelter or shade. Improper care can be given with lots of love. Peanuts might be so grossly overweight and have so much difficulty getting around even as a youngster that the consequences to her muscles and bones at an older age will be devastating. TinkerBell may indeed only like canned lobster and salmon from the most expensive labels, but the danger to her system from inadequate nutrition increases with each passing day. Queenie can be living with sores underneath the clumps of matted hair that bunch up behind her legs and ears and along her sides and flank because she so hates being brushed.

Since animals are unable to articulate their pains or difficulties, and since owner denial of the possibility of serious problems is all too common, it is not unusual for conditions that could be treated easily to go unattended. Perhaps owners fear that a diagnostic procedure will end with the veterinarian's suggesting euthanasia. Or perhaps owners postpone doctor visits when they finally notice that a pet has stopped enjoying life very much, hesitating to add in any way to the animal's stress. Because of owner denial, it is not at all unusual for a dog or cat to be brought into an animal hospital for its routine vaccinations quite a bit overdue, and for the doctor to find many decayed, infected, and fetid teeth, which can directly cause the development of serious heart and kidney problems. Reluctance to accept the necessity of dental cleaning and tooth removal may be so great as to have been the reason the owner stayed away from the doctor's office. The saddest part of that scenario comes from the fact that most pet-owner worry regarding dentistry is based on the incorrect assumption that chewing and digestion is the same in dogs and cats as in people. The human digestive process begins in the mouth; in dogs and cats it begins primarily in the stomach, and as long as food can be made small enough to swallow, it can be digested. Dogs and cats can eat normally and function well even if all their teeth are gone; in fact, it is better for them to have no teeth at all than to have a mouth full of the decay and infection that can lead to life-threatening systemic diseases.

The development of veterinary dentistry has saved many canine and feline teeth, jaws, and lives. Police dogs, like many others, are now receiving root canal therapy and prosthetic treatments that allow them to continue working. Techniques that were experimental thirty years ago are now performed routinely and refined daily.

Tumors are another source of denial even by caring owners. Lumps and bumps and even badly inflamed areas are "watched" in hopes that they will go away. Sometimes they do, but so many other times they not only do not go away but grow. During the period of watching and hoping, abnormalities spread that could have been repaired more easily and less expensively—and less disturbingly to the animal—if they had been dealt with sooner.

The G.s' mixed breed terrier, Mandy, weighed forty pounds. In time the fatty tumor under her front leg weighed almost five pounds. Although the tumor had grown slowly, her right elbow was pushed forward so far that walking was very difficult. The surgical procedure to remove the tumor took only thirty minutes, and within ten days Mandy was running and playing again. The consequence of the owners' waiting was discomfort for twelve–fifteen months longer than necessary; the result could just as easily have been much more serious and life-threatening, or life-ending. Ms. H. brought Bret, her 9-year-old Scottie, to the doctor in August, and explained that in May he had "gotten into the garbage one afternoon and seemed to have a swollen belly from all that he'd eaten." Now, four months later, Bret's swollen belly was sticking out two inches past his rib cage, and the six-pound cancerous spleen removed that afternoon from his abdomen may be the poster organ of denial! (Bret was very lucky: at any point, his grossly swollen and distended spleen could have ruptured, and the shock and consequential blood loss would have killed him in minutes.)

Today, there are many relatively new medicines and proce-dures, diagnostic techniques, and specializations in veterinary medicine and animal care, including cardiology, oncology, der-matology, radiology, neurology, ophthalmology, and internal and orthopedic medicine and surgery. The resources of these disci-plines are now available to the general practitioner for consulta-tion and referral, and the benefit to the pet-owning public is enormous. It seems ironic that illnesses, tumors, dental disease, and a whole variety of treatable ailments should be denied or ignored just because the animal is older. The same owners who thought that treatment was not necessary or important for natural conditions of aging are routinely delighted when their houses stop smelling dreadful from decaying teeth and when their dogs and cats start acting happy again after dental cleaning and extractions are performed.

Tumors and growths of many kinds are also often ignored until they reach monumental proportions, or until the growth impairs function, smells badly, or is bleeding.

Owners of aging pets who put off getting medical attention for their animal companions seem to be afraid that the doctor will say, "It's time to put Charlie to sleep." That would almost never happen: in the first place, the doctor wants to find a way to save Charlie as much as the owner does, and in the second place, veterinarians are very clear on the fact that final decisions about their patients reside with the owners. But the fear is real, even understandable: most of us are accustomed to look to the doctor for advice, and so often by the time pet owners actually steel themselves to hear a medical assessment, it confirms what their friends and family have already been telling them ("Look, Charlie's old, it's time to put him to sleep").

While sometimes potential expense has been a factor in the owner's putting off what s/he sees as inevitable, more often it is the fear of not coming home with the pet. Many practitioners make house calls in recognition of this very issue, realizing that owners feel more comfortable in their own homes, and less pressured to make any hasty decisions. When the veterinarian is able to recommend treatment or surgery, the owner usually, eagerly, agrees to it, vastly relieved to discover an unanticipated alternative to putting the animal to sleep.

It is sad when aging brings decline, but more age-related conditions can be treated than many people think. It is not unusual to have an aged animal brought into the animal hospital for euthanasia because the owners cannot bear to watch him struggle just to get around, yet medicines can be prescribed that sometimes will help greatly to improve the quality of that animal's life. Sometimes problems that seem monumental can be simply and effectively addressed by making basic changes in the type, timing, and amount of food supplied to the pet. For example, although Schatzie developed kidney problems, a reduced protein diet, inexpensive medicine, and some overdue dental work gave her and her family four more years of good times together.

There is, however, another side to the quality of life issue. While animal people are always interested in saving lives, and veterinarians take their training with that almost exclusively in mind, there does come a time when the rigors of daily living become too hard for our beloved pets and difficult choices have to be made. At the risk of anthropomorphizing, it seems appropriate to consider what the animal would wish for itself.

When Slick, a golden retriever, developed a painless neurological condition that made it impossible for him to walk because he could not support weight on his back legs, there was a device available that allowed his owner to easily hold up his back legs while Slick worked his front legs. This enabled his owner to say, "He's still having a good time; he goes to greet friends at the front door; we go out to get the paper every morning; and he's still ready to be anywhere there's a noise that means food!" That owner knew that if Slick could have explained how he felt he would have answered, "Sure, I'd rather be up and about, but this isn't so bad."

In contrast, when Boomer, a springer spaniel, developed an inoperable tumor in his stomach, and the only way to keep him alive for a time would have been by feeding him through a surgically-created opening in his stomach, it seemed clear to the owner that Boomer would have hated being as much of an invalid as that would have made him, and that euthanasia was the only choice.

Lastly, Sugar Ray, whose wasting disease took him from twelve pounds of sleek feline loveliness to three pounds of quiet sadness, represented an agonizing decision. He seemed to have no pain and he ate, although he derived little benefit from food; on the day after the family concluded that the quality of his life had become so diminished that the coming weekend would be their last with him, he took the decision away from them and died quietly in his sleep.

This is almost always what clients wish would happen when age and decline beset a beloved pet, but in those instances when it does not, the kindest thing a veterinarian can do is try to help them let go before the animal experiences pain and useless suffering.

7

Legal Issues

Laws dealing with the possession or protection of pets are relatively recent additions to the legal codes of most countries. While even as early as biblical times people were aware of the need to treat animals humanely, the reference was usually to work animals. The Old Testament described in great detail the ritualistic slaughter of animals for food, and Talmudic writings incorporated animals into discussions of dispute resolution and division of property. Aristotle suggested that since animals are incapable of rational thinking they are by definition inferior and subject to human rule. Common Law, the precursor to American law, offered little protection to pets and did not even specifically prohibit stealing them. Humane societies in Europe and in the United States originated in the mid-nineteen-hundreds, probably with the growing awareness of issues of individual rights and the abolition of slavery. Under current law pets are treated as property, which protects them from theft or destruction by others but not necessarily by their owners. Not long ago the state of Indiana addressed the question of how to charge a high school student who shot his dog to death so he could provide a body for biology lab. A recent ruling by a New York civil court judge stated that a dog is "somewhere between a person and personal property," and that in case of the animal's death "plaintiff's shock,

mental anguish, and despondency caused by the wrongful destruction and loss of the dog's body" could be considered.* Also
under current law pets have no rights to sue for damages or
directly inherit their owners' estates. Arrangements for pet care
after one's demise require designation of other humans as
trustees or heirs. *The New York Times* of July 13, 1996 reported on
a New Jersey Court of Appeals ruling that a dog emotionally
injured by teenagers throwing rocks qualified for payments from
the Victims of Crime Compensation Board; it is the dog's owner,
however, who will receive the money to use as she pleases (and in
this case the owner stated that she would use it to purchase
another dog).

Few people ever think of their pets in legal terms, but today
many aspects of animal ownership are regulated (see Gannon
1994). Current laws attempt to bridge protection for animals on
the one hand and protection of the rights of humans on the
other.

LAWS THAT AFFECT PET OWNERSHIP

The Health of Pets

These are in fact laws designed to protect the general public from
diseases carried by animals, such as rabies. (All states require
rabies vaccination for all house pets and many offer them at low
cost.) There are no laws addressing pet afflictions that have no
direct impact on human health, such as feline leukemia or Lyme
disease (though it is of course highly recommended to immunize
pets against them anyway).

---

*Cited in *Anthrozoös* 1996, vol. 9, p. 201.

Sanitary Controls

The pooper scooper law is by now widely accepted, and pet owners who do not clean up after their animals are considered social undesirables in most neighborhoods. The law clearly speaks to the needs of the public more than those of the animals, but the effect is to make pets less objectionable to those who prefer not to own them or be constantly reminded of their existence, and to reduce stress for all who live in cities and suburbs.

Restricting Entry of Pets

This is another category of laws designed to protect the health or at least the hygienic sensibilities of the general public. Most state laws prohibit bringing pets into restaurants; public parks are increasingly off limits to pets, especially dogs; and many hotel chains no longer welcome animals of any sort. The laws create problems for families wishing to travel with their pets but reflect a trend to restrict anything that can be considered even remotely hazardous to public health.

Travel Regulations

Getting from here to there has become easier only for those not accompanied by pets. Airlines welcome passengers and tolerate people's luggage, but they consider pets a nuisance and they demand extra payment accordingly. Using the law's definition of pets as property, they have regulations in place that limit their liability in case something goes wrong with pets in their care. Most pets survive air travel quite well (although stories occasionally make the news of pets getting loose during transport and ending up on the tarmac just as a jumbo jet is about to land). A cat was recently found in the baggage area of an airplane a week after disappearing from its cage, having logged some fifty thousand

extra miles. (No, it did not qualify for frequent miles.) If
something more serious happens the settlement entails limited
sums of money. For you the monetary value of your pet is not the
issue; for the airline it is the only one. Traveling with pets via
other modes of transportation is not any easier. Many bus
companies do not allow animals that cannot fit into a carry-on
bag, and traveling by car means finding places to eat and stay
overnight. The reality is that traveling with pets is getting harder
and harder and though there are some books out offering
information about travel possibilities with pets, you are likely to
encounter significant obstacles in just about any outing with pets
that is not merely a nature walk (and there are even trails,
especially around reservoirs, on which pets are not allowed).

Housing Regulations

Tucked away in the fine print of many leases is a "no pets" clause.
While it is often ignored by both tenant and landlord, it can
surface when the landlord decides to want the tenant to leave.
Many animals are given to shelters as the result of "no pets"
clauses in new leases, which have started appearing not because
landlords dislike animals but because they are legally liable when
a tenant's pet damages anything or anyone on the premises.
Sometimes the "no pets" clause can be deleted from a lease after
negotiation with the landlord, with proof that a particular pet
presents no threat to the safety or hygiene of other tenants. Such
an approach is clearly preferable to smuggling an animal past
doormen or hiding it from neighbors. A bill that would allow pets
for residents in public and publicly assisted housing has been
introduced to a congressional conference committee and stood a
good chance of passing.*

---

*Cited in *JAVMA* 1997, vol. 210, no. 10, p. 1392.

Animal Control Regulations

From time to time a suburban home owner insists on his constitutional right to keep seven pigs in his backyard in spite of his neighbors' objections; more commonly, neighbors complain about dogs that bark incessantly, somebody's pet snake finds its way into somebody else's laundry room, or a cat scratches up the entry hall carpeting in the wrong house. Many communities have animal control agencies or officers assigned to deal with such situations by negotiating a peaceful compromise. Although there are regulations that govern more stubborn problems, the legal system is reluctant to get involved; in fact, unless there is evidence that the problem presents a real danger or a significant public nuisance, the courts may mandate mediation. Pet owners should not be eager to go to court since judges are more likely to be sympathetic to the human neighbor's needs than to a pet's needs, especially if the owner is perceived as not having exercised appropriate control over the animal.

Property Damage Laws

Laws differ somewhat from state to state but as a rule owners are liable for the actions of their pets, so it is usually the owner who has to pay the price. (An important exception to this rule is when the animal has caused serious bodily harm and may be ordered destroyed by the court.) A law suit can be quite costly to the pet owner since in addition to legal fees he may have to pay for property damage, and punitive damages if the pet is a repeat offender. Law suits often stretch over an extended period of time, causing stress and delaying the prospects of resuming at least somewhat normal relations with the injured party. A few common-sense precautions will sharply reduce the occurrence of incidents leading to legal disputes:

1. *Every family should get to know the limits of their animal's tolerance.* If, for example, a cat is apt to become upset by such treatment as kids pulling her tail and to react not by escaping but by scratching the perpetrators, she should not be around young children unsupervised. The law distinguishes between first and repeat offenders, and the owner of a pet is at risk for heavier penalties if s/he is found to have ignored warning signs in the animal's past behavior. Knowing the limits of a pet's tolerance includes knowing how it handles new and unfamiliar situations. Rex, a dog of mixed breed, was found wandering the streets when he was a pup and was adopted by a loving family with whom he then lived his entire adult life. He proved to be loyal, affectionate, and generally relaxed. However, as soon as he was taken outside of his home he seemed to resume his lost-dog persona, acting suspicious of people and tolerating almost no physical contact with anyone. The owners quickly learned to be on the alert and keep him on a fairly short leash when outside: children were discouraged from petting him during walks and he was kept away from crowds or busy places. Taking the dog's unique personality into consideration avoided major problems.

2. *Owners should understand their pet's instinctive behaviors.* A dog running loose in the yard when the mailman has to get to the front door can be a setup for a negligence suit. A good fence, clear warning signs, and control of the dog's movements on the premises will save dogs from the consequences of their own actions. Other pets are less likely to attack visitors but can certainly do property damage, and it is vital to exercise pre-emptive control and good judgment in order to escape penalties if the animals do harm.

3. *Disputes involving pets should be nipped in the bud, regardless of who is at fault.* Accepting responsibility in the animal's

name and moving to resolve the issue beats adding insult to injury by blaming the person who was bitten, scratched or otherwise hurt. A situation that could be defused with a warning, a compromise, a settlement, or a handshake should not be dragged into court where expenses and passions can escalate.

Malpractice Laws

The introduction of law suits into the patient-doctor relationship is a growing problem in medicine, including veterinary medicine. Doctors usually do their best for their patients and patients usually put their trust in their doctors, but when things don't work out as planned the door opens for frustration, bitterness, anger, and malpractice claims. What pet owners have to keep in mind is that failure to cure does not constitute malpractice, and that gross misjudgment and incompetence leading to damage or injury has to have occurred in order for malpractice to be proven. If a veterinarian considers an animal to be too fragile for a complicated surgery and treats it with medication but the pet dies within a couple of weeks it is sad but not malpractice; if, however, the veterinarian overlooked a major health problem and the pet died within a couple of weeks—there could be reason to believe that incompetence was involved and a malpractice suit could be filed. The key is the degree to which a certain treatment deviates from acceptable professional standards, a determination that can be made only by other veterinarians (who serve as expert witnesses if the matter goes to court).

In a malpractice suit the owner can collect for any of three categories: (1) cost of fixing the damage done to the animal, (2) cost of replacing the pet with a similar one, or (3) punitive damages if the veterinarian's actions were inappropriate or unprofessional. While law suits claiming malpractice on the parts of doctors of human patients have yielded some astronomical awards for punitive damages, veterinary malpractice suits have to date compensated pet owners mostly for reparative costs or for the market value of a pet that died. Therefore, hope for large monetary awards should not motivate angry pet owners to sue. Those who are unhappy with the way their veterinarian has performed can turn to either the local veterinary association or the state licensing agency to initiate an inquiry; in extreme cases the veterinarian's license may be suspended.

Laws Prohibiting Animal Abuse

Public sensitivity to animal abuse has gradually led to the adoption of laws forbidding "unnecessary cruelty" or "neglect," and allowing prosecution for a wide range of abusive behaviors. Penalties for cruelty to animals have become increasingly severe, as in the case of the 1996 New Jersey law inspired by an incident in which a swan was clubbed to death as she guarded her eggs. Applying to all acts of cruelty to animals, the new law quadruples fines and imposes minimums as well as mandatory community service plus the possibility of imprisonment for repeat offenders. It is usually a complaint from a concerned citizen that leads to prosecution, though at times the police or a local authority become so outraged that no individual complaint is necessary. (Such was the case recently when dead and starving animals were found in a closed pet store whose owner simply abandoned them and skipped town.) In New York City public outcry followed reports that carriage-pulling horses were collapsing exhausted in the heat, and rules severely limiting their exposure in the summer were put into effect and strictly enforced.

The vast majority of pet owners are conscientious and provide at least adequate care for their animals. However, there are times when, without meaning to do harm, they fail to protect the pets from danger and so open themselves to claims of neglect. For example, a person left her dog in the car when she went to pick up a package in an office, assuming it would just take a minute, but the package wasn't ready and before she knew it half an hour had passed; she returned to her car to find an irate passer-by ready to call the police and accuse her of endangering the welfare of an animal. In another case a man was planning to go on vacation and asked a neighborhood kid to provide for his cat on a daily basis, forgetting to mention that it was an indoor cat. When the neighbor came to feed the animal, he left the door wide open and did not notice the cat meandering off; the cat, having no intention of running away, returned, only to find the house locked. After presumably meowing his head off for a couple of hours, the cat started wandering aimlessly and was hit by a car and injured. Somebody realized the owner was out of town and took the cat to the animal hospital—where he expressed his perception of the owner as guilty of neglect.

Even widely prevalent customs like cropping the ears or tails of certain breeds of dogs have come to be seen as possible violations of animal rights. Animal rights groups have vigorously campaigned for the discontinuance of what they describe as mutilation in the service of the frivolous esthetic preferences, and as a result many states have adopted fairly strict regulations as to who can perform such surgery and under what conditions. Gone are the days when pets were regarded as private property to be handled with no interference from others; under prevailing norms, the emphasis is on responsibility rather than possession, and therein lies a legal obligation to treat them well.

A concerned pet owner is likely to want to take action on witnessing someone abusing an animal. What can be done when a tough-looking guy is hitting a dog with a stick or a bunch of adolescents are throwing rocks at a trapped animal? Since people who enjoy beating animals might be so filled with rage that they could easily turn on other people as well, it is probably best to call the police or enlist the help of someone who could discourage any aggressive moves on the part of the abuser. If the abuser's identity is known, a complaint can be filed with the local Humane

Society, which is in position to launch an investigation, although of course it is always preferable to talk with the offender when personal safety and level of comfort permit.

PROVISIONS FOR SURVIVING PETS

The last thing that seriously ill or dying individuals should have to worry about is the continued welfare of their pets. The hope always is that a friend or a relative will adopt the pet and care for it as a matter of fact, but when there is reason to believe that no one will volunteer to do so, it is possible to create incentives and establish a system to address the problem. Step one is to try and find a reliable person or organization to take over if there are only a few survivors and none of them is in a good position to. Lawyers can help arrange to have the pet transferred to the adoptive caretakers and to have its expenses covered by the owner's estate for as long as it lives. The designated person(s) should know of the plans and also of the financial provisions, which should include monies for food, veterinary care, boarding during vacations, license fees, and miscellaneous extras. (A pet's welcome will be much warmer if it is not perceived as a financial burden.) It is of course impossible to predict how long the pet will live or how much care it will need. It is smart to assume that an animal will need more care as it gets older and that expenses associated with care will steadily rise. It is to be hoped that if a pet survives its owner by a long time, the new owner will treat it not as a guest but rather as his or her own. Generous provisions for a relatively young animal are still a good idea, though ultimately its welfare will depend almost exclusively on the good will of the adoptive caretaker(s).

The legal system has mostly avoided getting into the human–pet relationship, especially when pets were being considered property. As social sensibilities about pets have changed, however, some aspects of that relationship have become regulated. Pet owners remain free to love and to care for their pets without being burdened by concerns about the law. Common sense, courtesy, and the exercise of good judgment are usually all that is required. It is only when the wishes of the pet and the owner conflict with and impinge on the public good that legal considerations become relevant.

III

WHEN THE BARKING STOPS

OVERVIEW

The inescapable reality of life with pets is that their life span is usually shorter than that of their owners, and that at some point the vast majority of pet owners will have to deal with the loss of their pets. Such loss is due not only to old age but also illness, accidents, moves, theft, family circumstances, and neglect. At times the loss is sudden, at others it is anticipated for months. Some losses could have been prevented or postponed, others are beyond our control. But whatever the specifics are, the loss of a pet is a significant event in most owners' lives. For children pet loss is often the first encounter with death, mourning, and recovery; for young adults pet loss sometimes raises questions about the predictability of life; and for the elderly the loss of a loved pet tends to drive home the inevitability of death. For those owners who, regardless of age, have had a particularly strong attachment to their pets, the loss can be especially hard to handle.

Interpersonal communication is severely tested around the issue of pet loss. If euthanasia is considered, finding the right way to discuss it is a major challenge. Final decisions lie of course with the pet owner but here too listening to the sentiments of everybody can contribute mightily to family cohesion and strength. The same holds true for decisions about future relations with pets. It is quite common to find some family members eager to replace a lost pet right away and others who swear they will never ever adopt another animal. Interestingly enough, it is usually the children who request more time between pets, probably because the mere thought of another pet is equated by them with betrayal. Going with majority vote under such circumstances is not necessarily the best move; it is immeasurably better to try and reach a compromise decision that leaves no one feeling ignored or overruled.

If a new pet is adopted, especially if it is similar to the lost one, it may live for awhile under the shadow of its predecessor. If the last pet was overweight the new pet's diet will be carefully monitored. If the last one was hit by a car, the new one will be carefully, maybe excessively, restricted. Family members can help each other gradually separate the two and come to see the new pet as a unique and individual animal. Such a separation also frees family members from constantly living with the burden of painful memories. It is therefore a good idea to avoid naming the new pet after the last one or a variant of that name (like Willie 2 or Son of Sam).

When pet loss occurs grieving is a natural reaction. Even in the absence of established rituals for mourning a pet, most people find a way to go through the pain to emerge scarred but functional. The chapters that follow provide a conceptual framework for grieving as well as for readjustment, and explore the various resources available to those who find the pain too hard to bear alone, from contacts with the veterinarian through talks with the family to utilization of support groups or grief counseling. Once the immediate pain subsides the cycle may start again with the thought of having another pet. The moments in which the memories are still fresh but the yearning for a new pet experience is mounting are bittersweet. Life with a pet comes full circle at the point when consideration is given to offering another animal a new home in your dwelling and in your heart.

8

Unexpected Loss

Contrary to fantasies and wishes that prevail when a pet is adopted, life with the pet does not always proceed happily ever after. In fact, fewer than half the kittens and puppies that are brought into homes actually grow old there. The rest are either given away, die prematurely, get lost, or meet an unknown fate. At times careful plans are made to provide the pet a new good home, at other times the departure is sudden and violent. But for all caring pet owners the reality of the lost relationship is harsh and difficult to accept. When a decision whether to give the pet away has to be made, the process can be heartbreaking and conflicted, often pitting family members against each other and touching on a variety of other dynamics.

It is somewhat easier to part with a pet that never quite adjusted to life in a particular home than with a pet whose only crime was to trigger allergic reactions in one of its owners. But to the extent that the initial adoption of the pet was made with anticipation and out of free choice, the need to give it away, for whatever reason, often entails considerable soul searching and uneasiness.

Perhaps hardest to deal with is the situation in which the pet has to be given away not out of absolute necessity but as a result of another, sometimes unrelated choice. A somewhat common example nowadays is the person who has had a dog for some time and was able to care for it adequately, but is now offered a promotion that involves considerable travel. Friends or family can be asked to cover only up to a point, and eventually a decision has to be made regarding a more permanent solution. Another example involves two people deciding to live together whose pets cannot be trained to tolerate each other. At least one of them has to go, but which one? And yet another instance arises when the last of the children is leaving home and the parents, still healthy and adventurous, plan a full schedule of travel around the world. The dog is now 10 years old, the children want to see him when they visit, but they are in no position to take him. What to do? There are countless stories like these, none with an easy solution, yet people must find compromises that neither cut off their aspirations and needs nor neglect the welfare of the animal. It is important to leave oneself as much time as possible to find adequate solutions by spreading the word about the pet's availability and by using such resources as the veterinarian's office, animal welfare societies, the local paper, co-workers, and neighbors.

Less of a dilemma, but no less painful, is the need to give the pet away due to health issues, or non-negotiable reality factors. Such situations surface when, for example, an elderly pet owner moves to a nursing home or a single pet owner is seriously incapacitated. Just when the company of the pet would be particularly reassuring, it has, at times, to be withdrawn. And then there is the issue of allergies, probably the most common health issue forcing the removal of a pet from the home. One's affection and willingness to care for a pet whose presence triggers serious allergic reactions is severely tested on a regular basis. When the allergic reactions are truly serious and disabling, the decision to give the pet away may be painful but relatively clear. When the reactions are merely annoying, however, the decision becomes agonizing. After all, one may wonder whether just making one's life more comfortable is a good enough reason to give the pet away. What is at stake is not only the owner's physical well-being but also the way in which his or her decision will be viewed and judged by others who have an interest in the pet.

It is important, particularly in situations of choice, to maintain open communication among all family members and to tune in to feelings that may not be articulated but are manifested in certain behaviors (such as withdrawal, sarcasm, or preoccupation with other activities). For example, Mr. B., a dedicated family man and a father of two children, consulted a number of general practitioners, allergists, and veterinarians following the discovery that he had developed allergic reactions to the family cat. The cat was an affectionate creature, and both Mr. B. and his family were quite attached to her. But the medical consensus was that the only fully effective way to fight the allergies was to remove their source. This was an unacceptable proposition and Mr. B. embarked on a program combining medication with more limited contact with the cat, which was moved to the garage every day as soon as Mr. B. returned home from work. The program proved ineffective, however, and Mr. B. was getting increasingly prepared to seek a new home for the cat, sharing his thoughts with his family. A long period of protestations, arguments, and negotiations followed, in which it became clear that the disposition of the cat was only one of the issues involved. The children, failing to appreciate allergies as a serious medical condition, developed the notion that they too were disposable and could be shipped out for being a nuisance, and Mr. B.'s wife, who had gone through two difficult pregnancies and deliveries, was herself starting to resent her husband's unwillingness to tolerate some discomfort for the sake of family harmony. The practical solution eventually found was amazingly simple: the next-door neighbors adopted the cat and the children could visit her whenever they wanted to. The issues raised in the process were anything but simple, however.

There are many reasons that force a person or a family to

find the pet a new home, and the specific reason may have an impact on the search for an appropriate one. Even if the pet has been in the family for only a short period of time, its temperament and tolerance levels have been exposed so there is evidence on which to base the search for a good match. One would certainly not try to place a nervous or hyperactive dog with a family with very young children, for instance, or with an elderly or handicapped person. There are situations that may cause a dilemma as to how best to place a pet that has caused enough problems to justify its removal from one's home; there are not likely to be too many takers for an aggressive or untrainable pet, yet one may still feel a certain loyalty to it and a desire to find it caring owners. It is best to be direct about the pet's qualities even if doing so narrows the field of prospective takers, since owners who find out about these qualities the hard way are likely to be less generous and more punitive toward the animal, which behavior could lead to its demise.

Unexpected loss occurs at times when a seemingly healthy pet dies suddenly and without apparent cause. This tends to happen frequently with pets like goldfish, rodents, or birds, but clearly cats and dogs are not immune either. Pet owners who are faced with this kind of loss are left to ponder what went wrong, and what part they played in it. There is a sense of helplessness as developments unfold, followed by a search for answers. ("Did I neglect to notice something?"; "Should I have provided more (or less) of some ingredient in the pet's life?"; "Am I simply not meant to have pets?") In the absence of a clear explanation, the natural tendency is to blame oneself and feel guilty. Children are particularly vulnerable to such reactions since they always look for reason and order in their environments. Children's tolerance for ambiguity is fairly limited and they will find explanations, even if incorrect ones, rather than accept the fact that explanations aren't always available. For adults, too, reaching an acceptable understanding of unexpected loss is key to recovery.

A particularly painful form of pet loss occurs when a pet disappears or is stolen. The posters attached to utility poles in every urban and suburban setting are silent testimony to the prevalence of the problem. In a world in which children are occasionally kidnapped and adults are carjacked, the theft of an animal gets short shrift by the police, and efforts to locate and retrieve the animal are strictly the responsibility of the owner. Domestic pets such as cats and dogs do not usually intend to run away, so it is fair to assume when such a pet is missing for more than a day that something has gone wrong. More often than not the pet wandered too far and got lost or trapped, like the cat that wandered into a neighbor's garage, only to be locked in when the neighbor finished clearing his driveway and returned the snow blower to the garage, closing the doors behind him. He was found the next morning, cold and hungry but unharmed, when the owners heard him responding to his name during a neighborhood search.

In cases of pet disappearance, the first step should be a repeated search of the extended neighborhood, including questioning of local residents. (It's best to show them a picture of the missing animal.) Pets outside their familiar territories are particularly prone to accidents, so people should be asked about having seen or heard about any such thing. Only when search efforts fail should the possibility of theft be considered, whereupon it is well to remember that motives can be quite varied and it is not only pedigreed or exotic pets that are stolen. Some people take animals with the intent to sell them to pet dealers, even though most reputable ones will not buy them, and others hope to get the rewards for "finding" them (especially in wealthy neighborhoods). Some theft is impulsive, particularly that committed by youngsters, initiated with no clear plan as to what to do with the animal; chances for recovery of missing pets within a few days are quite good in those cases.

PROTECTING YOUR PET

While there is no guarantee against theft or loss of any sort, pets can be protected in some basic, essential ways.

Get Identification

All pets, even those who stay indoors, should carry some identification bearing at least their names and the telephone number of their owners. People who see a tagged animal wandering the streets are usually willing to make a phone call to the owner; they may not be willing to approach an untagged animal or to call the police or an animal shelter. A more sophisticated identification device is the implanted electronic chip, which includes information about the pet and its owners and can be read by scanners available to most shelters. Its biggest advantage is that it is still operational when the animal's collar has been removed. The implantation process is simple and is performed by a veterinarian with a local anaesthetic, and the device is gaining in popularity and promises to reduce the number of unidentifiable domestic animals.

Secure the Premises

Animals tend to be curious and follow attractive scents wherever they may come from and wherever they may lead; like young children, they do not seem to worry about finding their way back home, and they are apt to get lost as a result. Crawling through a hole in the fence is in all likelihood not an attempt to escape but rather a normal act of discovery: the animal simply takes advantage of what the environment provides, including ways to enlarge its operational territory. Therefore, it is crucial to have fences that clearly mark permissible boundaries and function as absolute barriers. (The same applies to electronic fences.) Besides avoiding ambiguity for the pet, clear boundaries discourage intruders, including uninvited animals.

Enlist Neighbors

Neighbors should be told if a pet is not supposed to be out alone, to avert the common assumption that it was intentionally out for a walk. As soon as a dog is acquired, neighbors can be informed that it is not to be outside unsupervised. Most people will respond positively to requests to alert the owner if a pet is observed on the loose since they provide an opportunity to be helpful without much inconvenience or effort.

Orient the Pet

Pets should be familiarized with the areas around their homes. Walking routines rarely change, as both dog and owner repeat them automatically. The problem is that as a result of such patterns only one area of the neighborhood becomes known to the dog and the next street over remains entirely foreign. Should the dog find itself unexpectedly alone on that unfamiliar block, it could easily feel disoriented and wander farther away from home rather than toward it. It is a good idea to walk the dog along different routes occasionally so that it develops a 360 degree map of the neighborhood.

Keep a Photo

Every owner should be sure to have a fairly recent, clear, color, full-body photograph of his or her pet. A picture is worth a thousand words, especially when it comes to describing a missing animal to strangers. Even if the owner can detail all the identifying features of the animal, a dispassionate stranger who saw it just once may not have paid attention to them. A clear, full-body photograph has the advantage of quickly registering in the person's mind and triggering either recognition or a blank. It is helpful to distribute fliers with the photograph and a phone number in case the person comes across the animal within a few days.

WHEN A PET IS MISSING

If the animal is not back in about 24 hours, quick action should be taken.

Prepare a Publicity Blitz

The more people know about a search, the better its chances of success. Posters attached to as many utility poles as possible are the most common vehicle for announcing a lost pet publicly. Such posters should relay key words (Lost, Dog [or cat, bird, etc.], Reward) so that they can be perceived in a glance. Many concerned individuals will make an effort to return a lost pet to its owners even if no reward is offered, yet the posting of one may serve as an attention-getter, a message that it pays to look at the poster or pamphlet. Children and adolescents may be tempted by a reward to actively look for the pet whereas they may ignore your search if there is nothing in it for them.

Any avenue that may publicize the loss should be explored, including relentless solicitation of such news media as local radio and television stations and the local newspaper. Ads can be placed in the "Lost Animals" section, but if the story can be given an unusually interesting or original angle (e.g., missing cat needs daily medication; lost dog belongs to a terminally ill person), it may be picked up as a news item and given considerable free exposure.

Man the Phone

It is unwise to rely on an answering machine, since some people are still intimidated by the device and others may not wish to leave their names or phone numbers; the person who does leave a message may not be available for a return call for quite some time. A direct phone conversation provides the opportunity to ask for details, to determine right away whether the found pet is the right one, and to arrange for its return pronto.

Contact the Local Shelters Repeatedly

Shelters are truly committed to the welfare of animals but they have to do a lot with very little. They will do their best to get the job done, but they will need clear and specific information that may best be presented in person, possibly more than once. Pets are sometimes brought to the shelters days or weeks after they were lost, and the shelter staff is not likely to review reports that came in earlier. When a pet is lost, nobody cares as much as the owner, who should not be afraid to be a nuisance.

IN CASE OF ACCIDENT

By far the most sudden and unexpected pet loss occurs due to accidents, usually involving automobiles. Such events are characterized by sudden shock from which one has to emerge quickly in order to provide urgent care for the animal as well as for others, particularly children, who may have witnessed or even been involved in the accident. Unlike illness, accidental injury does not allow for any emotional or logistical preparation, but if an emergency plan is in place, confusion and stress will be reduced.

- Pet owners should know where the nearest emergency veterinary care can be obtained 24 hours a day. Too often people rush their injured animal to their usual veterinarian only to find the office closed, but at any time, emergency services have the resources and equipment needed to treat serious injuries, as well as a staff that performs emergency procedures on a daily basis.
- It is important that taking care of one crisis does not create another. Accidents put extraordinary demands on all involved, and can be particularly traumatic for children who have witnessed them. Before parents scoop up the animal and rush to the hospital, children should be informed and assured of a call and a prompt return, babies have to be left with somebody capable of keeping them safe, the stove has to be turned off, and someone must be designated in charge. If the animal is injured to the extent that it cannot move on its own, it should be left in place to prevent further damage.
- Once the physical needs of the animal have been addressed the hardest challenge is dealing with the psychological aftereffects. Children are best served when they come away from even a traumatic situation having learned something, and what they may learn in a crisis are resourcefulness, responsibility, and recovery. Some of the learning will come as result of watching the adults around them, but some, even more important, will involve the discovery of adaptation skills that will be recalled for years thereafter with amazement and pride. Karen, for example, ten years old, was home with her father when the family dog, Pepper, was hit by a car in front of the house. The injury to the dog appeared to be very serious and the

father had to take action fast. As he carefully picked the animal up and placed it on a blanket in the car he told Karen to come along. The sight of the injured dog was too much, however, and Karen insisted on staying home until her father returned. There was no time for a discussion, and the father drove off to the veterinary emergency hospital without her. Left alone, obviously upset and scared, Karen nevertheless managed to locate her mother who was attending a professional meeting in a nearby town by calling large hotels and inquiring about meetings being held in their conference rooms, until she located the right hotel. She then had her mother paged, got to speak to her, and summoned her back home. By the time the father returned (sadly without Pepper) Karen was already being comforted by her mother, and the family was able to review the day's events with a mixture of grief and pride.

- It is entirely legitimate to feel exhausted from having relived the experience so many times and to need to create some distance from it.
- When a pet dies suddenly, there are going to be people who haven't heard about the death and who will cheerfully inquire about "the pooch." This awkward situation requires tact, sensitivity, and forgiveness, and if handled well can actually turn the exchange into an experience of interpersonal sharing.
- Concerned family and friends will want to know what, how, and why things happened. While at first such inquiry provides an opportunity for emotional release and working through the loss, the questioning tends to become intrusive.

PETS AND DISASTER SITUATIONS

Since pets live wherever their owners do they are likely to be affected by the same emergencies, crises, and disasters. Car crashes, floods, fires, or hurricanes leave owner and pet alike in a state of shock, suddenly removed from the safety of routine and forced to cope with the unfamiliar. Time is usually short and the owner may not have the luxury of searching for a frightened animal hiding somewhere. Quick decisions have to be made: Run back into the burning house to save the cat? Jump into the flooded stream to get the puppy? Reason may dictate one choice but emergency situations are never reasonable, and many people have found themselves acting heroically but thoughtlessly on such occasions. It is practically impossible to plan for all disaster situations but several commonsense precautions need to be considered.

> Pets traveling with their owners in any mode of transportation should be tagged. In case of unexpected separation the animal has a good chance of being reunited with the owner.
>
> When an emergency is anticipated (e.g., flood warning) all pets should be kept indoors or secured nearby. Frantic last-minute searches can and should be avoided.
>
> Cages or crates, clearly tagged and appropriate for all the pets in the house, should be readily available. When panicked, pets act unpredictably and may get lost unless properly secured.

The best hope that both pets and their owners have in a disaster situation is for the fast arrival of search and rescue teams. Professionals trained and equipped for emergencies bring with them a measure of organization and structure that is invaluable when the surroundings are chaotic. Rescue teams are trained in extricating the trapped and the injured, and in transporting them to safety. A guideline to local authorities was recently issued by FEMA (Federal Emergency Management Agency)* requiring for

---

*Cited in *JAVMA* 1997, vol. 210, no. 11, p. 1563.

the first time the development of emergency response plans that include animal care provisions. The activities included involve protection, care, and disposal (if necessary) of animal victims claimed by disaster.

Rescuers are aware that people in crisis do not make the best decisions, and they can prevent distraught pet owners from risking their own lives in futile attempts to save their pets. Rescuers take responsibility for what occurs on the scene, relieving the rescued of later guilt and self-recrimination. This is particularly important for children who may wish to throw caution to the wind, and who blame themselves for failing to save their pets. It is among the toughest parts of the job to decline the urging of frantic pet owners, young or old, to retrieve or to save an animal in need.

Admitting failure in rescue attempts is made harder in those cases in which rescue workers arrive with their own animals, usually dogs trained to locate life in the rubble. These working animals thrive on success and on the praise they receive when saving lives. When the disaster leaves few people alive, both human and animal rescuers are negatively affected. Rescue workers at the Oklahoma City bombing site had to cope not only with danger and exhaustion but also with what appeared to be increased stress in their dogs when they could sniff only dead bodies.

Disasters are to be survived and overcome. It is in retrospect that they may be viewed as intense bonding experiences that tested and reaffirmed mutual loyalty and commitment.

9

The Question of Euthanasia

From the humanitarian standpoint, the basic function of veterinary medicine is to extend the beneficial and enjoyable life of the animal patients and to prevent or reduce pain and suffering. When the animal patient experiences physical and observable suffering that animal patient may be granted merciful relief by man from its intractable pain or incurable malady.

The term euthanasia is defined as "easy or painless death" from the Greek *eu*, moving toward easily, and *thanatos*, death. The methods are designed to act promptly, painlessly, unalterably, and with a minimum or absence of conscious awareness of the animal. The most widely used products contain agents that in less concentrated amounts are used as a surgical anesthetics. Their intravenous injection renders the cerebral centers nonfunctional and produces cessation of respiratory, brain, and cardiac activity. What results is that life, as we can measure it, comes to an end.

When restraining the animal in preparation for the injection is apt to cause pain or stress, prior tranquilization can make the entire procedure easier for all involved, including the owners, who are usually surprised by how fast the drugs work and how calmly the pet responds.

Although recently there has been some debate over the terminology: "Put to sleep" rather than the more accurate, but far harsher: "Put to death," the usual euthanasia is, indeed, more of a "putting to sleep" as the animal quietly loses consciousness.

The decision as to who remains in attendance and who does not is often as difficult as the euthanasia decision itself. Most caring owners feel that the family, or a family representative, must be with the animal in its last moments, yet the distress of temporarily inconsolable owners only adds to the pet's confusion. Therefore, there are times when it is easier on the pet to be left in the hands of the veterinarian and staff, who have learned to maintain calm in the face of sadness and death. A final family good-bye and a hug before the actual euthanasia, sometimes leaves the animal with less apparent anguish.

A seldom-discussed consequence of family pressure during the procedure is that the first thing people remember when asked about their beloved pet is the euthanasia. It is not necessary for owners to experience anything but the *life* of their pets. Most families are relieved to learn that their attendance neither impacts on the veterinarian's opinion of their caring for the animal nor does it help the animal itself. Veterinarians do not always agree on the question of family attendance; indeed, some veterinary hospitals prohibit it. To the extent that there is choice, there has to be information about what to expect, followed by contemplation. Unfortunately, few people welcome discussion about any aspect of euthanasia when the matter is not imminent, so preparation and reflection are usually limited.

The O.'s were a typical family with eight raucous children, who loved Buster, their boisterous Lab, with a fierce and enchanting intensity. When Buster reached 12 years old, laboratory examination of blood and urine samples showed him to have a mild kidney problem. The promise that medication and diet would help him for a good while did little to relieve the family's anguish, until it became clear that they were wondering about what their choices for Buster would be later on but were afraid to ask questions about euthanasia lest the veterinarian think they were considering doing it immediately. Their ignorance had led them to envision all sorts of strange scenarios. Learning that the drugs act quickly and painlessly, and that there are choices for cremation and burial, prepared them to make the final decision when it came to be time.

Some individuals will succumb to worry if they do not at least view the animal's remains because they want to be sure that the body of their pet is not going to be used for experimental purposes. The fear is as widespread as it is unwarranted, although there have been reports of unscrupulous laboratories and cemeteries. It is continually surprising to most practitioners to discover how much their clients fear "experimentation" following euthanasia. The reality is that there is no conceivable gain, financial or scientific, that any lab could achieve from randomly experimenting on aging or ill or badly traumatized animals.

The fact that the life span of most household pets is substantially shorter than that of their human family members means that people can expect to face the question of euthanasia more than once. It is usually the first experience that is the most difficult, the hardest for which to prepare, and the one that may influence all future experiences of pet ownership. For most people, the very thought of ending the life of another being, especially a beloved pet, is extremely difficult, yet privately, they wonder and wish they had the courage to bring up the subject of euthanasia. Pet owners commonly make appointments for long overdue vaccinations when they really want to consider euthanasia. The animals appear very ill, or with one or more large growths or other serious maladies. As often as not, the owners have inadvertently put off asking the euthanasia questions until euthanasia has become the only reasonable choice.

The timing can sometimes be almost as thorny a problem as the decision itself. Logistical, economic, and emotional factors come into play. The advent of house call practices has made it easier to deal with a 100-pound golden retriever suffering pain on any movement, or a large German shepherd in renal failure throwing up bile, or a non-declawed cat with a bleeding mammary tumor and no tolerance for the cat carrier, but then coping with the actual bodily remains of the euthanized animals presents a new logistical problem.

Financial considerations are, sadly, a real problem. As medical costs escalate in the human communities so do they in the veterinary field. While advances in veterinary medicine offer many more options, most practitioners are realistic enough to recognize that economic limitations may preclude their full utilization.

Pet owners need to ask sooner for advice even when they are fearful of what the answers might be. Early discussions can yield clearer options and understanding, and it is wise to establish certain criteria BEFORE emotionally wrenching conditions occur. Discussing the reasons and signs that would lead to euthanasia, or the consideration of euthanasia, can almost always be easier when that decision is not imminent; ethical and moral and psychological issues can be discussed with professionals in veterinary medicine, psychology, and religious disciplines when there is time.

QUESTIONS TO ASK WHEN CONSIDERING EUTHANASIA

- Do we have a veterinarian who knows us and our pet?
- Do we know for sure who is available and when?
- Would the family prefer that the procedures be done at the animal hospital or at home?
- How will the pet be transported to the hospital and by whom?
- Is there a house call practitioner in the area?
- Should the pet be sedated first?
- What are the hospital or house call hours, and what are the policies and procedures for handling the pet and the remains?
- What is our part of the procedure?
- Is there an optimum time of the day for the family—a

quieter time at the hospital? A time when the children will be gone, or be home, or back from college?

- Does the family want a simple cremation? Can the cremation be individual? Can the ashes be returned? A country or cemetery burial? Is it available? What does each of these cost?
- Does the family want the pet to be buried at home? Does the town have ordinances against that? Is the season of the year suitable for a gravesite to be dug? Who will attend?

10

Grief and Bereavement

And she had little dogs she would be feeding
with roasted flesh, or milk, or fine white bread.
And bitterly she wept if one is dead
or someone took a stick and made it smart;
She was all sentiment and tender heart.

Geoffrey Chaucer, *The Canterbury Tales*

Embedded in Chaucer's lines is the recognition that the nature and intensity of grief are intrinsically related to the kind of relationship that existed before the loss. A pet that was pampered and loved will be greatly missed and mourned. In fact it is the emotional investment in the pet that will define the emotional reaction to its loss. As was hopefully made clear in the section on attachment, there is a close relationship between what we put into a relationship and what we have to endure when it is disrupted.

The way each one of us grieves, regardless of intensity, is a result of personal, cultural, and social factors. Every society provides rituals and customs designed to help the bereaved deal with loss. But there are many losses that are not regarded as fully legitimate and are therefore not associated with socially sanctioned bereavement practices. A remarkable book, *Disenfranchised Grief*, by K. J. Doka, lists the various losses that in our society do not meet the criteria for legitimacy and so leave individuals suffering such losses isolated and bewildered. Included among them is pet loss, a kind of loss often considered marginal and undeserving of meaningful grief. But as every bereaved pet owner knows, the grief following pet loss is not only very real but also very much like grief reaction to any other highly significant personal loss. Recently, a religious service for loss of a pet was proposed by a Virginia veterinarian who is also president of her congregation.*

Most of our knowledge about grief comes from observations and studies about people grieving over relatives and friends or preparing for their own deaths (Kübler-Ross 1969). The few published works on pet loss borrow from those studies, implicitly acknowledging that grief follows pretty much the same sequences regardless of what is actually grieved.

When we ask what grief means we don't really expect a definitive answer as much as a greater appreciation and under- standing of what comes with it. Grief is a given of human nature, an experience which transforms our lives by incorporating death and loss. Sadness and crying are only the initial expressions of grief, the emotional signals that a deep psychological process has begun. Even people who have a hard time crying (mostly men) experience an emotional reaction to loss that can be quite profound. In fact, grief is such an overwhelming experience that those who have studied it have either regarded it as an illness from which one is expected to recover, or as an adaptive process that follows a number of distinct phases that somehow allow better comprehension and maybe a sense of control. The two models are not necessarily contradictory in that both agree that in the midst of grief our adaptive skills are severely tested and we are vulnerable to varying degrees of disorganization, despair, and illness. It is not the amount but the quality of grief that changes

---

*Copies of this service may be obtained by sending a SASE to: Ruth Chodrow, D.V.M., P. O. Box 375, Fischerville, VA 22939.

over time. Elizabeth Kübler-Ross is probably the best-known authority on dealing with death, and her classification of phases involved in death and dying has become the literature standard. It is important to note, however, that her five proposed phases (denial and isolation, anger, bargaining, depression, and acceptance) refer to preparations for one's own death rather than to the death of someone else, and are not entirely applicable when the death has already occurred. Grief over the loss of someone else can take one from the original attachments through their loss to new attachments. Grief is not only a reaction to the past; it is also a bridge to the future. Let us review some principles that apply to all grief reactions.

The first thing to remember when dealing with grief is that the process is not linear (first denial, then anger, then bargaining, etc.); there is no proof that every individual even goes through the same stages (Corr 1993). Grief may be strong or weak, brief or prolonged, immediate or delayed. The way we grieve as individuals is influenced not only by what we have lost and by the circumstances surrounding the loss but also by our past experiences. There is no right way to die or to grieve, no correct path, no formula. For the grieving person there may be comfort in being able to identify and to recognize some feelings that others have described, but also there may be anxiety when the subjective experience is different. For example, most conventional descriptions of grief do not mention relief, yet the bereaved might well be relieved that a prolonged and difficult situation has finally come to an end. Many pet owners watch helplessly as their pets deteriorate, wishing for the end to come soon, yet unprepared to euthanize. When death finally comes it may be experienced as a relief, though often mixed with guilt over having wished for it. Our emphasis on sorrow restricts the range of socially acceptable reactions, so the experience of relief can expose us to unnecessary and unjustified guilt and shame.

The function of grief is to allow individuals to recognize the loss and to integrate the reality of loss into their lives, to swallow a pill that is not only bitter but is also perceived as having no curative value. As such, grief is (at least at the beginning) an elaborate protest, which enlists for its purposes one's entire experiential world. Loss and grief mean different things to different people but they are generally experienced on a number of levels—the physical, the emotional, the spiritual, and the cognitive.

REACTIONS TO LOSS

Physical

A significant loss almost always leads to disruption of sleep patterns either directly (the mourner is too upset to sleep) or indirectly (regular routines have been disrupted). Deprivation of sleep tends to make people nervous, grumpy, and even more depressed than they would otherwise be. It also makes any recovery that much harder. It certainly isn't harmful to have a sleepless night once in a while, but sleeplessness catches up with us very quickly, so steps should be taken to overcome persistent disturbance (taking mild medication, returning to a normal sleeping schedule, avoiding overstimulation, and doing something relaxing before going to bed). Loss also often affects our appetites and eating habits and our usual sense of physical well-being. We can all withstand changes in eating patterns on a short-term basis, but fairly quickly such changes make us nervous and disoriented. The sooner we return to more or less regular eating the faster we regain our sense of constancy and order. The same holds true for exercise routines, which are among the first to be disrupted when we are upset. Lastly, loss fosters a certain sloppiness: we tend to allow a superficial mess around us (not make the bed, not dress properly, not replace a burned-out lightbulb). We say we are too upset to attend to such unimportant concerns, yet the sloppier we permit our environment to become, the more depressed we are likely to feel. The way people take care of their bodies and of their surroundings is a fairly good indication of how solidly connected they feel to the world around them.

Emotional

Much of the drama of loss and grief occurs on the emotional level. Initial anger ideally gives way to eventual acceptance, but all too often anger persists as the dominant emotional reaction to the unfairness of loss, and it becomes the background on which bitterness, irritability, and inability to sustain relationships are played out. More than almost any other emotion anger can become all-consuming, and seriously impact our normal interpersonal exchanges. Anger and depression are two sides of the same coin, both contributing to the breakup of our social and interpersonal support systems and fueling our perception of the world as a truly inhospitable place. Add such a perception to the pain of the original loss, and the potential for damage of letting anger and resentment go unchecked is apparent. Holding on to anger, even if its origin is legitimate, will advance neither change nor escape from an unpleasant state of mind. Someone may indeed have been responsible for the accident that led to the demise of a treasured pet but no amount of blame and anger will bring the pet back. We can be angry and depressed or we can move on in life but not both. The sooner that realization sinks in the faster the restoration of a productive self. The way to defuse intense anger is usually to articulate it as openly as possible and also to be open to such alternative emotions as compassion, empathy, generosity, and forgiveness. It is not at all uncommon for anger to lose much of its punch once verbally expressed.

Spiritual

Nothing has the capacity to shake one's faith in God (or whatever higher power one believes in) as much as the loss of a loved one. Even nonreligious people ask "How could this be allowed to happen?" when they struggle with the unfairness of loss, especially when it is sudden and tragic. What gets rattled is the somewhat naive notion that in return for our faith we will be spared unfairness or injustice. But such a contract exists in our heads only, and it reflects wishful thinking about somehow being protected and the assumption that somebody else is responsible for all that goes badly in the world. It is hard for us to reconcile faith with death even when intellectually we understand the ways of the physical world. We know that death ends everybody's life yet we also hope for some reprieve due to our faith. It might be helpful to conceptualize faith as a belief system that we may use to sustain us through good times and bad, to reflect our own strength and resourcefulness back to us when we most need it. When a loss produces profound feelings of abandonment, faith can provide a sense of belonging, first in terms of spiritual connection, later in relatedness to others.

Cognitive

Making sense out of loss and death (indeed of life itself) has been challenging man throughout history, and generations of philosophers have struggled to find coherent explanations. Chances are we will have to wait many more generations before a satisfying explanation surfaces, and in the meantime it is up to each of us to come up with a personal philosophy of life and death. Luckily we are not completely in the dark since, whether we know it or not, we live our lives with a set of assumptions about the world and understand events in our lives accordingly. Some people see the world as a stage on which they can make their mark: even a loss is regarded as an opportunity for creative adaptation, bringing out personal resources and flexibility; others see themselves as cogs in a large machine with little or no self-determination and therefore no capacity to adjust to changes. Most of us are probably somewhere in the middle of this continuum, but all of us faced the need sometime to come up with a way to continue dealing with life without despairing. To the extent that we can find meaning in what we have in life we must tolerate the idea that we cannot have it forever.

One of the typical features of grief is that it starts as an overwhelming ache and evolves into recurring painful pangs. These are moments of intense hurt in which some memories flood our consciousness and disrupt the calm facade we are somehow able to create. What was lost returns in vivid color, but with it comes an awareness that the return is imaginary, not real. Certain as we are that the dead do not come back, our minds continue to struggle, to protest, and to search to retrieve the loss. (Pets, especially dogs, seem to act on a similar principle upon the loss of their owners.) Such efforts are rooted in a pattern existing since infancy of seeking security and continuity in our environment. The pangs of grief are the concrete expressions of this search, but they also serve as steps toward recognition of its futility.

Grief does not start upon death but rather upon the realization that the current condition will in all probability lead to death. The concept of *anticipatory grief* was coined to refer to the psychological preparation for someone's death, including the planning (before), coping (during), and reorganization (after) that accompany the awareness of inevitable loss. Anticipatory grief usually unfolds almost secretively since in many circles openly discussing impending death is considered bad form, as if talking about it may actually bring it about. (People have a corresponding aversion to discussing wills and organ donations.) Anticipatory grief implies that in bereavement one gets to reevaluate one's entire history with the deceased and, in so doing, to reevaluate quite a lot about oneself. When a pet dies we get not only to recall the good times we had with it but also to rethink our place in the pet's life and in other people's lives. Were we good owners? Do we give enough of ourselves in our relationships? This process starts before the pet dies and goes on for a long time after the worst of the mourning is over.

In grief we react not only to the death but also to the deprivation that the death brings about in terms of the emotional supplies that are no longer available. We miss not only the animal but the entire complex of interactions with it that gave the relationship its meaning, what the animal embodied and stood for in our life. When a pet dies the physical loss is mourned first, but deprivation of the relationship quickly becomes the more painful experience. We can all relate to the sharp pain that can emerge even years later on walking in the woods and wanting to throw a stick for Rover or noticing the dandelions that were the favorite snack of our guinea pig.

THE EXPERIENCE OF GRIEVING

In general grief triggers a number of experiences loaded with personal meanings.

- **Sense of loss.** Even if a pet was not the center of its owner's universe, its loss may be perceived as quite central to their existential world, at least for a while. Only after losing something do we realize how much we depended on it for our feeling of stability. The silence following the doorbell's ring can be a disturbing reminder of a dog's absence and how much we miss it, even if we used to always yell at it for barking so much.
- **Generality of loss.** Grief takes over our emotional land-scape. When we are missing our pet we are sad in general,

not just about the pet. The sadness spreads like a dark cloud over our lives and becomes the filter through which everything is seen; we feel depleted of all energy and spirit. Children no longer enjoy summer camp when they learn that their pet has died back home, and adults go through the motions of work preoccupied with thoughts of their loss. The death of the animal raises questions about the meaning of life and about fairness and commitment, and more.

- **Review of life.** The recollection of shared moments is an integral part of grieving for a pet, and of course what we review is not just the life of the pet but our lives as well. We may smile at the memory of doing something extraordinary for the pet, frown at recalling an incident of neglect, and appreciate once again the richness of the experience. Years of shared experiences are often compressed into a comprehensive, timeless set of memories.

- **Going through motions.** A bereaved person does not fully participate in the world around him, but acts more like a detached spectator or like someone acting a role no longer relevant or authentic. S/he continues to function in the world but without much sense of involvement or investment, surrounded by thick fog that prevents real contact. Strains in relations with others are not at all uncommon during the period of bereavement, and the potential for isolation is quite serious.

- **Sense of unfairness.** Though we understand the reality of death we may nevertheless consider it unfair that a sweet, loving, gentle animal has to die, especially prematurely. And since nobody has a good answer to the big questions we are stuck with our frustration and the anger related to it. We may feel singled out for unfair treatment, and our belief in the benevolence of God may be tested at such times.

- **Lack of control.** One of the scariest elements in grief is the

awareness of lack of control. There is simply nothing we
can do about death (other than possibly rush or delay it
somewhat), and when we encounter this reality in its
starkest expression we may feel intense fear, even terror, as
when the foundation on which we stand is trembling
beneath us.

- **Struggle to contain the loss.** The immediate reaction to
  loss may be so intense that we may need something to
  counterbalance it. Since we are all driven to survive we
  automatically attempt to contain emotional damage done
  to us (as our bodies do in response to physical trauma). As
  humans we try to evoke our sense of agency, our ability to
  feel that we have something to say about our fate. At our
  disposal lie psychological defense mechanisms such as
  denial of reality but also adaptive mechanisms such as
  putting things in perspective and giving ourselves time to
  adjust. By holding on to what has not been lost we manage
  to contain the despair that might otherwise overwhelm us.
- **Appreciation of others.** When we are able to turn to those
  around us for support we may be better able to address all
  the dangers described above. We also may see in some of
  those around us certain qualities of which we may have
  only been dimly aware, such as unusual kindness or
  capacity for empathy. We particularly appreciate those who
  make themselves available to us and who do not demand
  that their needs be taken care of at that particular time.
  Many deep and lasting friendships have emerged from
  periods of grief. When others share the misery (as in a
  bereavement), the mutual support is invaluable.
- **A new understanding.** After the tough questions of fairness, anger, and loss of faith are raised and contemplated,
  grief often leads to a new intuitive understanding of
  relationships and their place in our lives. Accepting the
  reality of separation due to death may lead to enhanced
  appreciation of relationships while they last. Awareness of

the possibility of loss can actually trigger more of our generosity and availability. We are likely to be more patient and tolerant once we have dealt with the pain of separation and acquired a new appreciation of relationships.

- **Thoughts of the future.** In the middle of grief the future looks bleak. Not only are we engulfed by sadness over the loss but there is nothing in the vision of the future that promises a reprieve. We don't want to even imagine a new attachment to another animal; the thought of loving another pet feels remote or maybe indecent. Gradually, the vision changes, however, and we actually find relief in knowing that we have maintained our ability to love and to care.

- **Developing a readiness to let go.** With time the pain tends to become duller and the pangs of grief less intense; we get ready to embrace the entire experience of loss and grief as an integral part of ourselves. Grief does not end abruptly; rather, there are turning points, recognized mostly in retrospect, when the sharp pain gives way first to a duller ache and then to a sense of acceptance and readiness to let go. At times such turning points coincide with other events such as a move or an anniversary. At other times they seem less linked, and more sudden. The person who has suffered grief is a changed person. He is a more complex individual with a few more layers of experience and adaptive skills, and does not simply go back to being his old self afterwards. Events are no longer taken for granted, nor are relationships or attachments. The price may be a permanent shadow of sadness, a tear close to the surface when memories come flooding, but with it appears a greater tolerance for all that life has in store. Grief does not disappear; it fades in intensity, leaves center stage, allowing life to continue.

- **Grief as a marker.** After a pet dies we may recall events in relation to the time of its death, and memories in general may be stored on either side of that event, before or after (e.g., "we bought this couch when Spot was still alive"). This is another indication of how our lives change as a result of death and grief.

When grieving we are looking for others who can relate to our frustrated dreams, our pain, and our anger about our situation, even when we know our reactions to be unrealistic or unfair. But in reality we are likely to run up against a certain stigma that the role of mourner often entails. Primitive societies used to isolate the bereaved from their peers, believing that any contact would lead to more death. Our society is more tolerant but the bereaved are still treated with considerable unease and at times avoidance. Mourning is confused with weakness or self-indulgence, and the attention given to the mourner is therefore a mix of sympathy and pity.

In our society, and probably in most others, men, by and large, have been found to grieve differently than women do. At the risk of overgeneralizing, it could be said that men typically internalize their sadness, remain silent, become aloof, and resort to driven behavior and hard, often physical work. They seek to stay in control of themselves and their surroundings, and may take steps "to do something" about the situation, which may include drinking, striking out, or looking for someone to blame. Women, on the other hand, express feelings of vulnerability more openly and expose their grief somewhat more directly. The freedom to cry in public, to offer and receive physical comfort in the form of hugs or embraces, and the willingness to share verbally are great assets during emotionally demanding times. Women seek support groups and professional help in far greater numbers than men, precisely because the mode of operation in such settings plays to their strength.

It should now be clear that grief does more than bring the bereaved full circle (back to the starting point). Grief is concerned with more than surviving; it leads one to a modified appreciation of life and therefore affects all future relationships. In spiritual terms one might say that grief enables us to reach a more enlightened existence, a revelation of aspects of our nature we have been unprepared to acknowledge, a wisdom of experience that reminds us of what we could be, should be, and sometimes are. We do not choose to experience grief, but once we are in its grip we are in the unique position to extract from it the raw material for further personal growth.

11

Children and Loss of a Pet

One of the saddest moments in many children's lives occurs when a loved pet dies. Because of the intense attachments that develop between them, children respond with considerable alarm to any threat to their pets. From chasing away a neighborhood cat that hisses at their own to sleeping on the floor next to a dog that seems to have a belly ache, children put themselves on the line for their pets and tend to assume personal responsibility for their welfare—even when they neglect the daily responsibilities of feeding, walking, or cleaning. This loyalty is an important building block for other relationships, although it does create problems when the pet's condition deteriorates in spite of the child's tender loving care.

The loss of a pet is the first real encounter with death for many children, who cannot avoid exposure to scenes of death on TV news and in cartoons, video games, and the movies. Graphic as such scenes sometimes are, they do not trigger the kind of heartache that comes with watching a loved pet deteriorate or die. Though not as permanently damaging as the loss of a parent or sibling in most cases, the death of a pet is a severe psychological challenge to a child. Such a first encounter with death ideally enables the child to develop coping mechanisms that will prove useful in the face of future losses, some of which may be more severe and traumatic. Existential anxiety, a constant and normal companion in childhood, makes close encounters with death highly charged and puts the child's coping skills to the test. Children look for personal meaning in everything, and when they struggle to deal with sad, previously unfamiliar events they are in danger of reaching erroneous conclusions that open the door for self-blame, guilt, and misunderstanding, which in turn can have far-reaching implications for behavior and adjustment.

The experience of loss in childhood, especially when traumatic, carries with it many more risks in terms of later disturbances in development. The way children respond to a particular early loss determines the way they are likely to respond to losses in the future. Of particular significance is the fact that it is not always the loss itself that leaves its traces but the way adults accommodate the child's emotional reaction to the loss. When there has been no previous encounter with death there is no way to be prepared for the emotional reaction to it. There may exist a general fear or anxiety in anticipation of it but no knowledge about how to deal with it and no way of even knowing whether one could survive it. Things are particularly scary the first time around, especially when one can pick up the apprehensions and fears in others as expressed in hushed voices, meaningful glances, or, worst of all, silence.

Children respond to loss differently from adults. At different ages they have different capacities to grasp the concept of death and devise ways of handling it. Even preverbal children have the ability to grieve for a person or an animal to which they were attached. The grief may not be in the form of extensive crying or overt sadness, but rather in a continuous struggle to deny the finality of the loss. Infants and children continue to act as though preparing for the return of the lost pet or person, and any anger or rage gets expressed only much later, when the realization of finality hits home. It is then often directed at those perceived responsible for (or even merely associated with) the loss, or at those perceived as hindering the recovery of the lost object. Responsibility in this connection may derive from having caused the loss in some way or from failing to have prevented it. It is of critical importance to clarify the precise reasons for the pet's death in order to minimize the development of unnecessary guilt. The availability of a caring and stable support system is crucial to enabling the child to go through grief and emerge safely.

In the context of family life death of a pet is one of those events that if handled well maintains family functioning but if mishandled can have lasting effects on family ties, trust, and security. Few other events bring together so many elements of what a family is all about as the struggle to deal meaningfully with death. What is tested at such times is not only each person's resourcefulness and ability to withstand pain, but also the ability to turn to others for comfort rather than blame, to allow oneself to appear vulnerable in front of others, and to look beyond the loss. While an individual's natural inclination may be to withdraw into a private grief, the family is challenged to limit the withdrawal and offer an atmosphere that invites more open expression and allows more effective processing of the loss. Just when the pain is most acute family members are called upon to reach out to each other, to receive as well as to give emotional support, and to demonstrate their family loyalties.

Children, lacking a larger perspective, may be more seriously affected by pet loss, especially when the animal is identified as their pet. Parents are then expected to provide perspective, to place the loss in a manageable context, and to walk the children through the grieving process. This is probably the trickiest phase of dealing with death since everybody is hurting, tempers tend to be short, blame is easily hurled at others, and defensive reactions just make matters worse. Parents don't always have the patience to deal with the death of a gerbil as a major trauma, but if they appear too cavalier about it they fail to appreciate the meaning of the loss to a child. It must be remembered that what is lost is not just the gerbil but also some security, predictability, and control. This is clearly no small matter. What the child needs at such times is the perspective on life and death that the parents have achieved, which encourages a belief that in the end things will get better.

As is the case with any mishap, pet loss can bring even remote relatives together. Extended families often bemoan the fact that they get together only at funerals, that busy schedules and routines keep them apart; when a pet dies the opportunity to reconnect on a somewhat less tragic occasion presents itself. People are unlikely to fly across the country, but phone calls and letters are meaningful contacts, always appreciated. (Hallmark's cards expressing sympathy for pet loss have been a great hit with people looking for just the right words on such occasions.)

Undoubtedly, the best way to deal with the death of a pet entails the involvement of all family members. If the loss can be experienced as a family loss rather than as one child's loss, the experience can actually serve to enhance family cohesion and offer strength to all its members. Misery indeed loves company, and if it is the company of those closest to you so much the better. Parents in particular have to establish and maintain a delicate balance between the opportunity for grieving on the one hand and the need to go on with life on the other. If this is the first loss in the family the children will turn to their parents for clues as to how to handle the situation, and they will attend not only to what the parents say but also to their mood and emotional presentation. It is wise for the parents to turn similarly to their children for clues in order to assess their needs at that moment. Questions should be encouraged and explanations provided in the most straightforward manner possible, but requests for private time to mourn should be respected as well. Parents know the emotional styles of their children and should take them into account when dealing with pet loss.

JASON'S LOSS

Jason, an 11-year-old boy, the only child in an intact suburban family, was referred for psychological counseling due to difficulties in social adjustment noticed by both the parents and the teachers. A capable student and a good athlete, he was nevertheless only marginally involved with other children, showing little interest in developing friendships or participating in group activities. He did not appear overtly depressed but there was no humor, no enthusiasm, no expressed optimism. He spoke intelligently and coherently but in what seemed to be a lifeless manner. His description of his family environment gave no hint of any mistreatment; the parents were characterized as hard-working individuals who spent most of their free time at home. When asked who else lived in the house Jason answered that nobody did, but there was an edge to his voice, suggesting that there was more to the story. An inquiry about recently deceased family members yielded nothing, however, and the conversation shifted to other issues. The theme that emerged was of the unreliability of relationships and of life as a whole, quite surprising considering Jason's stable home. It was only when the therapist persisted in trying to understand the source of his outlook that Jason mentioned a dog he "used to have." Asked to tell more about the dog, Jason, for the first time, appeared unwilling to talk, saying, "He is probably dead, that's all." What gradually emerged was Jason's belief that the dog was killed at the local shelter after it was given away by his parents. Though he said he understood his parents' reasons for giving the dog away, his response seemed to reflect his characterological compliance more than a genuine acceptance. It became clear that Jason was harboring considerable pain as well as anger related to the loss of the dog, but that he did not feel free to express any of those feelings to his parents, who handled it all so matter-of-factly. Instead he internalized a conviction that things come and go, and that emotional attachments are therefore too risky. Jason never had a chance to explore and articulate his many questions surrounding the dog's departure, including the parents' ulterior motives, possible alternatives to the shelter, follow-up to ensure that a good home was in fact found, and the emotional impact of the entire affair on the family. The painful feelings were suppressed and what was shown to the outside world was the emotional withdrawal and the loss of hopefulness. The good news was that a relatively short period in counseling (including a few sessions with the parents) created a space within the family structure for raising these suppressed questions, expressing hurtful feelings, and mourning more appropriately for the dog.

HELPING CHILDREN COPE

The following points should be remembered when helping children cope with the loss of a pet.

1. The loss of the pet represents the loss of an important relationship, no matter how the rest of the family feels about the animal. (Children are fully capable of revealing their deepest secrets even to a pet inchworm.) The loss must therefore be acknowledged as meaningful and should under no circumstances be trivialized, even if the child's initial reaction is nonchalant. It is not uncommon for children to present a blank facade that can be misinterpreted as indifference or as no emotional reaction at all when anger or bitterness is clearly part of the experience. Similarly, children may appear to return to a normal routine rather quickly, yet the loss continues to have its impact in subtle ways and to be detectable in drawings or in dreams. Even if the child never did seem very attached to the pet the loss can still be meaningful, because the death represents not only the end of that animal's life but the fragility of all relationships.

2. The child should be free to feel a wide range of emotions, including some that other family members think are strange or inappropriate. No one holds the absolute truth about how grief should be expressed. It has to be experi-

enced in accordance with each individual's character and state of mind. The child is not helped when advised not to cry so much or told to act in some prescribed manner. Grief is a sad but creative endeavor, on which an individualized stamp has to be imprinted. Many adults are disturbed to see a child who has just lost his pet play with his friends in an apparently carefree manner, but it would be a mistake to remind the child of the lost pet or of the need to grieve for it. There is little danger that the loss is indeed forgotten or the grief foregone. It is simply that children follow their own gut feelings in dealing with trauma and are less burdened by convention and by a need to act a part.

3. Children can move quickly from one mood to another. They can be in tears one moment and engage in a lighthearted conversation the next. Adults may be fooled into believing that the tears, therefore, were not genuine, and the grief not real. The rapid transition from one emotional presentation to another is in fact an adaptation to the danger of being emotionally overwhelmed, and is no reflection on the depth of the emotions experienced. Children should not be encouraged to stay with the sadness or to express it in a way that is more understandable to adults, unless it becomes clear over time that continued suppressed grief is inhibiting their normal functioning.

4. One element of respect is truthfulness, and as in any other aspect of the relationship with a child, honesty must be encouraged. Too often children are exposed to misrepresentations, or even to outright lies when adults consider the truth to be too embarrassing or difficult. In fact, children, who are in the midst of learning how things work in the world, crave the truth, and are profoundly appreciative of those who present it to them. If the truth is unbearable, children have highly effective psychological

mechanisms to cut down on its impact and to process it gradually. This is not to say, however, that facts should be thrown at the child without appropriate preparation. The child's age, maturity, temperament, past experience, and available support system, as well as the nature of the events all need to be taken into consideration. Those who know the child are in the best position to assess what s/he can handle and to offer additional guidance and support when needed. Encountering death for the first time, the young child has to deal not only with sadness but also with a new fact of life of which s/he had no previous knowledge, and it is up to concerned adults to make their struggle as straightforward as possible. In general the younger the child the more concrete the information has to be in order to minimize misunderstandings. Every psychologist can testify to the frequency with which individuals in therapy report the long-term effects of childhood events that were poorly—or never—explained. Adults may have the best intentions when they hide a difficult truth from children, but secrets rarely remain hidden for very long and when they emerge distorted, denied, or rationalized they cause more damage to the relationship than the truth possibly could have. Besides, children will blame the adults more for being dishonest than for what they say.

5. Communication with children is filled with euphemisms, which serve mostly to reduce anxiety levels of the adults. It is particularly tempting to resort to euphemisms when discussing death, and they may in fact make it possible for the topic to be broached altogether. There is probably no harm in speaking euphemistically or metaphorically as long as it is absolutely clear that the child understands the reality behind the coded speech. Children's perceptiveness and common sense should not be underestimated. The story is told of a mother who, in an effort to spare her

child's feelings, told him that the dog was now with God, to which the child responded: "What is God going to do with a dead dog?" In an appropriate context most children can handle hearing "the dog died" rather than "the dog was put to sleep (or went to heaven)," and direct talk is preferable. But explaining euthanasia, for example, to a young child may require some translations or even omissions in order to prevent unnecessary anxiety. (The adult may want to be very clear about the procedure but a young child might wrongly apply the concept of mercy killing to himself or to those he depends on and feel anxious when sickness occurs.) When possible, precise and objective terms should be used when discussing the death of a pet, but the adult speakers have to be comfortable with the language they use and should express themselves in a way that addresses their own anxiety as well as the message they are trying to bring across. Children learn to hear the nuances in their parents' speech and can get the picture even if the language is vague. In the end it is the atmosphere in which the communication takes place that matters more than the precise words used.

6. Children can be helped not only by the caring adults around them, but also by other resources such as friends and books. Always attuned to input from peers, children respond to sympathetic messages from their friends, in whom they are likely to confide their feelings to begin with. Acceptance by peers assures the child that the loss, great as it is, is limited to the pet and does not affect the rest of the child's life. Sharing the grief can in fact cement friendships and provide a stronger sense of truth in others. Books offer a less personal support but they do provide the child with assurance that others have gone through similar loss and have survived. The fact that those others have found the words to articulate their grief can

serve as license to do the same with family, friends, and teachers. And speaking of teachers, modern schools often have classroom pets to which the children may get quite attached. For a variety of reasons these pets usually do not get to live very long and teachers often use their demise as a way to discuss the issue of death. Such lessons, when taught with sensitivity and compassion, provide a good frame of reference for more personal losses. Among other things the child learns that not everyone is an animal lover, and that not everyone is deeply moved by such loss. But the child also learns that many others appreciate the meaning of life and death, and those are the ones to whom s/he may turn when seeking empathic sharing.

7. Any death, including the death of a pet, creates a sense of helplessness. Children are particularly affected as they tend to be excluded from whatever efforts are made to save the pet before its death, and often are not involved in any relevant decision making (such as whether to operate or to euthanize). Depending on the child's developmental stage it can be very useful to include the child in dealing with the dying animal in whatever way the child is comfortable with, be it keeping track of medication, shopping for required equipment, or simply providing tender loving care. Opportunities should be offered but the child should not be made to feel guilty for declining them. Some children find it too emotionally draining to be around animals (or people) they are about to lose and prefer to detach themselves as much as possible. Such behavior carries with it some long-term risks (being out of touch with one's own feelings, for instance), but being forced to act against one's inclinations may be even more damaging, especially to the sense of security and protection within the family. Pressure to act compassionately is doomed to failure since compassion has to come from within, free and spontaneous. The child who pulls back

from a dying pet should be encouraged to express his or her feelings and conflicts, but whatever choice is made should be accepted. Lectures on responsibility can certainly wait for a more opportune time. Once again the adults who know the child are in the best position to assess his or her ability to actively participate in preparing for the inevitable loss.

12

Following the Loss:
"I Will Never Have a Pet Again!"

The period immediately following the death of a pet is characterized by continued absorption in the animal in terms of arranging for disposal of the body, discussing the loss with others, and planning memorialization of some sort. Some of these activities are done in private, others involve sharing. The veterinarian is often the first person consulted regarding decisions that have to be made, and the veterinarian has the facility to hold on to the pet's body until a final decision is reached by the owner. Regardless of the owner's choice the office can either arrange for the transfer of the body to another facility or for its disposal. Most veterinary clinics have lists of relevant local resources.

As is the case following any other personal loss, the desire is to establish lasting reminders of the deceased, express one's most tender feelings, and gain support from others. And yet there are no guidelines and only a few conventions regarding such memorials for pets.

Memorials may range from small keepsakes associated with the pet such as a name tag, a collar, or a food dish, to more elaborate items such as a gravesite and headstone. Other forms of memorialization may include donations or volunteering at animal shelters, and writing in memory of the lost relationship. (Some of the world's best known poets and writers have published moving testimonials to their grief upon the loss of their pets, and touching expressions of contemporary grief can be found on the internet at The Virtual Pet Cemetery @ www.lavamind.com/pet. html.) The way a grieving pet lover chooses to memorialize a pet is entirely individual and depends on the choice between maintaining concrete or abstract ties. For many people burial in a cemetery, and the opportunity to visit a permanent grave, is the only real option. A burial ceremony can be individualized, allowing owner and friends to express their feelings in any ways they wish, and the burial site could be linked to a memory forever associated with a certain pet (such as a stream where dog and owner would often go fishing) in preference to the traditional pet cemetery. For many others the best memorial is within their memory. Cremation may then be the choice, and the ashes may be kept or not. It is important to note that since there are only few legal restrictions on the disposal of the pet's body the decision is truly yours and yours alone, even though we all become very emotional at the time of loss and do not always feel comfortable making decisions.

It is a good idea to ponder the question of disposal of the pet's body before death actually occurs so as not to be pressured to make a decision at a highly emotional time, and all but the very young should have a voice. Among the issues to be considered in search of a solution that most family members can live with are: legal restrictions (if any) to burying the pet on family property; the likelihood of moving away soon, inhibiting visits to the burial site; the expense of burial—in the thousands when all is said and done; current level of comfort with decisions made when pets died in the past. The family should seek to live free of guilt and shame with its choice, which, it is hoped, reflects authentic feelings about the pet and the relationship to it. People should not be swayed by the untrue notion that an animal's remains will be turned into pet food unless they are buried in a pet cemetery, or be talked into elaborate, expensive schemes.

It is important to be particularly sensitive to the needs of younger family members to say goodbye to the family pet. Even when they deny strong feelings, the adults should provide for an open expression of sorrow about the loss. One effective way of doing that is to hold a ceremony or a memorial service that simply notes that the pet played a role in the family's life and that its absence will be felt. Exercising some control in a situation that is mostly outside our control helps us maintain some sense of order and safety. The children can determine how elaborate the service should be and they can take an active part in it by writing, drawing, or reflecting on their lives with the pet and their feelings at the moment. Speaking at a service may provide participants an opportunity to reveal anecdotes and stories that were not known to others, enriching the memories of everybody and reinforcing a sense of closeness among those present.

GETTING ANOTHER PET

The idea of getting another animal following the death of a beloved pet is one that will most likely surface before long. This subject is practically taboo in the initial phase of grieving, when the permanence of the loss is only starting to sink in. Before long, however, the bereaved starts encountering the expectation to get over the loss. Getting over it is not always the point, and adopting a new pet is not always the answer. The period following the death of a pet is a good time to think and evaluate choices; there is certainly no point in rushing into action on the rebound. If and when the longing for animal companionship proves stronger than the disposition to avoid a new attachment, the next step is to assess getting another pet.

   Is the ability to fully love another pet in doubt because the pain of the loss was so great? No one is in position to fully enjoy the gift of a new pet if he or she is still consumed with pain. Lost things almost inevitably become idealized, but by recalling all aspects of life with the lost pet we can produce a memory package beyond idealization that can adequately integrate love, sadness, anger, and other feelings. Have the rewards of pet ownership been greater than the sacrifices? Are there other people involved whose feelings and opinions should be considered? Even if there is agreement in principle on the idea of getting a new pet, there may still be significant differences as to such details as what kind to get and when to get it. Finding out what others think and want should be done sensitively and slowly, taking care to avoid creating pressure, guilt, and tension. Mr. E. responded to what he believed to be his wife's need by arranging a visit to a shelter. His wife was not in fact eager to adopt a new pet so quickly, but suspecting that her husband's gesture reflected a need of his own that he could not articulate she agreed to go. It was on the way to the shelter that they both confessed to considerable ambivalence, and they decided to postpone the adoption until they were truly ready.

The pain involved in losing a pet can be severe, but out of this pain considerable good can emerge. Successful grief work releases the capacity to love again, which in turn enables us to risk future losses for the benefit of new attachments. When the promise of a new relationship outweighs the risk of future pain, people are ready to reconsider the decision never to have another pet. Probably the greatest obstacle to such a transition is guilt at investing in a new relationship as though it betrays the lost one. It is sometimes difficult to combine the deep yearning for what was lost with the search for fulfillment in a new relationship. Most people are probably ready to get another pet when:

- They miss the things they shared with the lost pet more than the pet itself—the routine of feeding a cat in the morning, talking to a bird, or taking a dog for a walk in the park. That is the point at which it seems a new pet would be genuinely welcome, not as a substitute but as a new provider of old pleasures. (A friend related how she woke up one morning, reached out for her dog as she had for years, and realized that finding a dog, any dog, at her fingertips was a real need. That was the moment she knew she was ready to adopt a new one.)

- They can look at other people's pets without immediately and automatically thinking about the pet they lost. When we can genuinely appreciate the beauty and uniqueness of individual animals we are likely to be open to new possibilities in our own relationships with pets.

- They catch themselves reading pet-related ads in the newspapers or stopping to look at posted offers of pets for adoption. Our minds work in mysterious ways and sometimes we find ourselves doing things we never quite planned on doing. This is one way in which questions emerge into consciousness that were ignored or suppressed until now.

- They feel they have love to give and a new pet could benefit from it. Anyone who can mourn for a lost pet but at the same time also love and nurture another should, by all means, feel free to do so.

- Above all, they don't feel disloyal to their old pet for considering having a new one; indeed, they don't doubt the genuineness of their feelings toward either pet. When we can care unconditionally about a new pet while at the same time remaining sure of our love for the pet that died, we have crossed an important threshold and are ready to move on.

Once people have decided to adopt a new pet they still have to decide whether to get the same breed again or even the same species. While "cat people" may consider only felines worthy pets, others will be open to experimenting with alternative kinds of love. Maybe a cat was the right choice for a single person rarely home during the day and often out at night. Now, ten years later, there are two young children in a house that is rarely empty plus a partner who really prefers a dog. Or after having had a dog it may be time to go back to gerbils so the kids will have a pet of their own. Or after retiring, when too many chores would be burdensome, mightn't a cat be the perfect pet?

Families with young children tend to adopt young animals that are temperamentally compatible with, and certainly more tolerant of them. The house is pretty chaotic anyway, so why not add a rambunctious puppy? Besides, the family just dealt with a loss, and a young pet is not likely to die soon and subject the family to loss again. The situation is quite different in households that do not include young children, particularly where the desire to have a pet is balanced by the need to slow down or the inability to move around a lot. Adopting an older animal may then be the right choice even if it means a less certain future together. Such a pet may arrive set in its ways and less willing to be molded and trained, but probably very appreciative of the love it once enjoyed and is now offered again.

Many people who have had pets find it difficult to imagine living long stretches of time without the company of animals; for them the decision to adopt a pet following a loss is very easy. Others decide while their pets are still alive that they like animals but no longer wish to share their homes with them after this one; for them, too, the decision may be easy. But for still others, maybe the majority of former pet owners, the decision-making process is complicated. The important thing to keep in mind is that adopting a new pet is the easy part; choosing to care for the animal for years to come is the real decision.

13

When Recovery Is Hard

The cultures that prescribe rituals and customs for grieving (mostly for human losses) also prescribe lengths of time for them. The Jewish custom of Shiva, for instance, designates seven days of intense mourning. Ancient Roman society imposed a quarantine (from the Italian "forty") on mourners. But the goal of transcending the loss may still prove elusive since there are no clear guidelines as to how to do so, and there are great individual differences in how people deal with loss. We often observe and evaluate the behavior of others in terms of how we think we would handle similar events in our lives. Our own reactions are the norms by which we judge others to determine in our own minds how "normal" their behavior is. Even so, we are usually able to distinguish socially standard responses to loss from those that are extraordinary. The differences may be not in the behavior itself (e.g., crying, social withdrawal), but rather in its intensity, duration, and form.

PROLONGED GRIEF

An individual may find it extremely difficult going through the grieving process:

- When the loss was particularly traumatic. Loss is always tough but losses that are sudden or violent or involve much suffering are particularly difficult to overcome. Every time the loss is recalled the person is reminded not only of the animal now gone but also of the traumatic circumstances surrounding its death. That was the case with Mrs. W., whose dog drowned in her swimming pool while she was in the house. Her family became alarmed and sought professional help when, throughout the summer and the fall following the accident, she was visibly depressed, refused to go anywhere, and did not respond to any efforts to console her.

- When guilt is too strong. Guilt is a powerful, unpleasant, yet almost unavoidable reaction to many situations that end badly. And when it comes to the loss of a pet there are in fact instances in which the death or the injury that led to it could have been avoided. The grief-stricken person who knows that s/he bears some responsibility may be inconsolable by family, friends, or the veterinarian. Ideally people have the capacity to forgive themselves for mistakes, neglect, even some abuse of their animals, but in reality guilt may be so strong as to prevent forgiveness or compassion. Grief can thus become prolonged and unresolved.

- When the attachment was particularly strong and involved dependency on the animal. Dependency is not the same as love. Love allows the participants to be free as individuals whereas dependency binds them through obligations. Pets, by definition, depend on their owners (at least for sustenance) but when the owners depend on their pets or live in symbiotic relationships with them, separation is experienced as intolerable and grief work designed to facilitate the separation is blocked. A rather common example of such dependency is the situation in which the relationship with the pet compensates for the absence of genuine intimacy in a human relationship such as a marriage. Numerous women who have shown excessive reactions to the loss of their pets have spoken of miserable marriages and unsatisfying relationships with their families, from which they sought and found refuge in their interactions with their animals. One woman described her lost dog as the only living thing on which she could depend.

- When no other important attachments exist at the time of the loss. What often makes it tolerable to deal with death is the comfort one gains from other attachments. If none exist, the pain cannot be shared, the sadness feeds on the loneliness and isolation, and the recovery is made that much harder. When the loss of a pet is the last in a chain of other significant losses, it may be experienced as the last straw and trigger powerful reactions of despair and hopelessness. Mr. D., a man well in his eighties, managed to cope with the death of both his wife and his son several years earlier but was in complete agony following the death of his cat. He had often talked about the cat as his last remaining family, and had shared with it the kind of intimacy from which all others were excluded. In fact, for the four years Mr. D. outlived his cat, he remained somewhat aloof from those around him. Loss almost always triggers yearning for the past, which at times of grief always seems better than the present. If the past was in fact a considerably richer period in the person's life, any losses that further impoverish the present are that much harder to deal with.

- When considerable ambivalence existed in the relationship. Children are occasionally afraid that by wishing someone dead they may actually bring the death about. This reflects fear not only of their omnipotence but also of their ambivalence, since they usually direct their death wishes at those whom they both hate and love. If such wishes do come true the grief is tinged with guilt and responsibility, making recovery harder. But children are not the only ones to experience ambivalence in their relationships with others. Remember the young woman from Chapter Two who inherited her dead mother's cat? The ambivalence toward the mother was transferred to the cat and the love-hate feelings were so strong that the eventual death of the cat plunged this woman into emotional turmoil from which she had difficulty emerging. Most relations with pets are not ambivalent; indeed, it is the very absence of ambivalence that endears pets to their owners. Some mixed feelings may emerge at times even in these relationships, however, as when the animal has become a burden due to ill health, for example, or costs. It may seem perfectly legitimate to forego expensive treatment for a sick older pet and to feel annoyance at the burden of the conflict involved, yet when the pet dies shortly thereafter, the awareness that medical interventions were available can contribute to a more troubled grieving. For that reason people should try to resolve conflicts and ambivalences while the pet is still alive.

By comparison, those who recover well usually have extensive support systems, opportunities to openly express their grief, and time to recall at length and at will their experiences and related feelings. Family members, including children, can be part of the healing process, and friends of someone who has just lost a pet can also help.

HELPING SOMEONE WHO HAS LOST A PET

The grieving person is likely to be fully aware that reality has changed. Pointing to objective reality rather than sharing the person's current subjective experience of it actually distances the would-be supporter from the grieving individual. In fact, it is another's willingness to address feelings of sadness and loss that helps the bereaved feel more comfortable with his or her own grief. Similarly, the other's willingness to acknowledge the full impact of the loss is liberating for the bereaved. The exchange immediately following a death is difficult in that there is no formula or prescription for it once the conventional sympathy has been expressed. The awkwardness derives from the fact that the consoling friend cannot help the bereaved by bringing back what was lost and the bereaved cannot help his or her friend by seeming less bereft. It is the contact and the knowledge that it is genuine that provides the most comfort.

A statement like "I know what you are going through" can doom an attempt at empathy, because each experience of grief is quite different. Pet owners see their pets as unique, and so do they see their losses: someone else may know what it's like to lose a cat but not what it's like to lose Tiger. Asking the bereaved to talk about his or her experience recognizes the legitimacy of that unique grief.

Statements like "Such is life" or "He had a wonderful life" are somehow dismissive of the depth of the loss and imply that the grief should be diminished. A rationalization like "At least she no longer suffers" is an attempt to put a positive spin on a negative event and implies that the pet owner should rejoice rather than grieve. There is truth in the words but it is important not to let this truth overshadow another truth—that a life has been lost. It is probably better to encourage the mourner to recall some shared experiences even if they trigger tears since the sadness will then be mixed with warmth and relatedness. Even anticipated losses must be mourned, and rich and pleasant memories are simply no substitute for grief work.

Sterile as some of these statements are, they reflect a genuine desire to alleviate the suffering of the bereaved. It is better to resort to clichés than to ignore or dismiss a fellow being's experience. You are not expected to solve anybody's problem, but simply be available, supportive, and accepting.

Those who wish to help must recognize that pain is an inevitable part of the grieving process and that it must be expressed and shared to be overcome. This recognition means offering a quiet yet supportive presence, lending a hand with daily routines, listening to expressions of feelings, but refraining from unsolicited (and usually unproductive) advice. The grieving person may be concerned that his or her expressions of grief are too intense or inappropriate, and the supportive presence of a caring friend can supply much needed reassurance. Such a friend may be just detached enough to assess the general state of mind of the mourner and to gently suggest interventions if the grief threatens to put the individual in some sort of danger. Relatively few people intentionally harm themselves in reaction to loss, but many create potential problems through carelessness, preoccupation, or neglect. The fact that visits are appreciated in spite of the sense of helplessness shared by both the bereaved and the visitors is testimony to the power of sharing and communicating. Even if nothing of practical value is said during the exchange, the visit is likely to have the positive effect of reminding the bereaved that not all is lost, that even in bad times others can be counted on. The greatest threat at the time of loss is that the bereaved will feel alone—which is precisely why visits and other forms of contact are so beneficial.

SUPPORT GROUPS

There are times when the closest people are too involved (or involved in the wrong way) to be good candidates for sharing the feelings of a mourner. Family members and even good friends may be too invested in a quick and smooth adjustment to the loss and a return to the way things used to be. People less intimately connected to the bereaved, whose personal agendas do not present a burden, may be able to offer the kind of listening and responding that contributes to clarity rather than add to the confusion. Support groups fall into this category and their popularity attests to their special contribution. They are sometimes led by professionals (psychologists, social workers, veterinarians) and sometimes by lay persons who have a particular interest in the process, usually as a result of personal experiences. The underlying principle is that shared sorrow is easier to bear than sorrow experienced in isolation. The emphasis in these groups is on sharing not only the loss and the attendant feelings, but also the uniquely personal solutions and adaptations that individual members have found useful. A camaraderie tends to develop that is similar to what grows among survivors of any battle. Members of such groups maintain friendships long after their participation in the groups has ended. The chief benefits of membership in groups are:

- Maintaining contact with other people. Support groups are open and new members join as old members depart (or stay). The opportunity exists for meeting new people and maintaining contact with them outside the group, counteracting the common tendency among bereaved individuals to isolate themselves socially. Even when the substance of the group discussion seems to have little value, the fact that it involves talking and interacting with others is significant.
- Meeting people with similar experiences. Group members establish a somewhat exclusive club in which there is refuge from pretense and from having to appear composed. Group members can offer each other modes of support and comfort that neither professionals nor strangers can offer (e.g., embraces, hand-holding, shared weeping, etc.). And group members commonly feel really understood in the group, connected to relative strangers as to very few others.

- Finding a forum where expressions of grief are in fact welcome. A common fear among bereaved individuals is that once they let out their emotions there will be no relief from the pain, but group members quickly come to see that crying spells rarely last more than ten minutes before the body, exhausted from the stress, actually relaxes and the crying stops. The fear of emotional expression often turns out to be worse than the emotions themselves. Also, since everyone in the room is in some emotional distress, members are just about assured empathic listening and support.

- Utilizing the experience of others to devise personal forms of adaptation. New group members meet others whose losses occurred some time ago and who are already on their way to fuller recovery. Being witness to such a process is therapeutic in itself and helps the bereaved to start putting their loss in some sort of perspective. For example, members who are further along often talk about whether to get another pet, a subject that may appear irrelevant to new people but does provide some vision of the future.

- Learning to shift the focus from personal grief to that of others. After only a short time group members are bound to encounter someone whose loss is more recent, whose pain is more acute. Know-how in dealing with the initial shock and pain of the loss and in utilizing the support of the group to start the recovery process is the best thing to offer the new member, and sharing it actually provides a chance to feel more in control.

- Learning about volunteer opportunities. Being in a group, especially one led by a lay person, could easily inspire someone to become a volunteer. The awareness that out of misery some good can come is an inspiring thought that has propelled many individuals into activism in various areas. In the field of pet care there are endless opportunities for volunteer work, all highly rewarding. The work can be hard and demanding, yet few other activities are more gratifying than helping animals in need.

PROFESSIONAL HELP: THE VETERINARIAN

The veterinarian's role as a front line professional dealing with loss usually starts well before the loss actually occurs. Pet owners expect care that is not just proficient but compassionate as well, care that will include attention to psychological and emotional reactions of owners as well as to medical problems of the animals. The vast majority of veterinarians fulfill such expectations not only because they are caring individuals but because a more complete and comprehensive care is the centerpiece of modern veterinary practice.

The veterinarian can help by providing information about procedures, choices, and the range of human reactions to them. S/he will listen to concerns, answer questions, and possibly assist in reaching decisions. No major medical intervention will take place without the informed consent of the pet owner, and the entire exchange will occur with the understanding that both parties have the best interests of the animal in mind. However, the reality of a busy practice makes it impossible for the veterinarian to provide the kind of psychological attention that many pet owners require when their pet is seriously ill or dies. The veterinarian is sure to be sympathetic and supportive but not necessarily prepared to deal with anything but the most basic expressions of grief.

In situations of considerable stress the likelihood of misunderstandings and misinterpretations increases dramatically. It is not uncommon for distraught pet owners to become edgy, to deny what the veterinarian is trying to say, and to ignore treatment recommendations. An experienced veterinarian will take such behavior in stride, recognizing the difficulty of the situation and allowing the pet owner to reach decisions when s/he is ready. Even when the frustration leads the owner to misdirect his or her anger toward the veterinarian, a patient and tolerant stance will probably defuse the situation quite quickly. It is important for the veterinarian to remain candid and direct even when the owner appears scared and anxious. A balance between truthfulness and gentleness must be attempted in an effort to protect both pet owner and veterinarian. When it becomes clear that the pet owner is seriously distraught the veterinarian is likely to offer help by referring to a mental health professional. This is neither an abdication of professional responsibility nor a suggestion that the owner is psychologically impaired; rather, it is a recognition of the intense strain that the pet's condition is putting on the owner's coping ability, and the provision of an effective tool for dealing with it.

The role veterinarians play does not have to end with euthanasia. If the owner wants the animal's remains following cremation, for example, the opportunity exists for further discussion about the loss as well as about future options. It is always in the interest of both veterinarian and pet owner to maintain their good relationship in spite of the pet's death. In fact, the relationship could become a determining factor in the client's decision to adopt another pet. When the time comes the veterinarian, having known the client's bond with other pets, is in a unique position to advise what sort of animal might be particularly suited to this individual or family. The veterinarian may also know owners who for one reason or another are trying to place their pets in new homes, and can therefore serve as a liaison, assuring both parties of the animal's health and safety. Just about every veterinary clinic features a bulletin board on which pets for adoption are posted together with other announcements of interest to present or past pet owners. Some clinics sponsor educational discussion groups or bereavement groups, encouraging pet lovers to maintain involvement with animals even while being petless.

PROFESSIONAL HELP: THE THERAPIST

There are times when the bereaved individual (or couple or family) seeks professional help in dealing with what appears to be complicated grief, a reaction to loss more intense, more devastating, and more prolonged than either the person or those around him consider acceptable. Admittedly such a definition is subjective, but grief is a highly subjective experience. We all know when we act in a way that does not fit in with our self-perception, or when those dear to us act out of character; when the gap between our reactions in a given situation and our self-image is too wide for comfort, it is time to consult with a professional. Members of a family respond quite individually to loss and no adaptation appears to please everyone. Father wants to be left alone, mother is in tears and doesn't want to do anything, one child keeps asking questions, the other has resumed wetting the bed. In most instances a brief intervention of several sessions is enough to reestablish normalcy in the household, and to identify one or more family members who could benefit from additional psychological assistance. It is not at all uncommon to find that the loss of a pet catalyzes the rise and expression of dormant family tensions as the family struggles to cope. The therapist is in a good position to help family members articulate the factors contributing to tension and to offer ways of handling them. If all goes well the crisis is resolved without anyone feeling blamed for this or other family crises.

Complicated grief, for which one would seek professional help is not a clearly defined phenomenon and could manifest itself in a variety of forms. Generally speaking the complications occur either because there appears to be a significant lack of visible grief (avoided grief), or quite the opposite—chronic grief that shows no signs of being worked through. In either case the absence of an open expression of grief and hope results in inability to eventually make new emotional investments and in significant blocks to recovery. Depressed behavior, which may follow unresolved grief, may not be recognized as related to the loss but instead be construed as tiredness or exhaustion. It sometimes takes professional intervention to clarify how unresolved grief can color the entire experience in living. Such was the case, for example, with a middle-aged woman who continued to be the solid anchor for her family following several losses in a few years. She did not become moody or withdrawn as one of her daughters did, she did not take sick time or personal time from her rather demanding job, and she seemed to maintain her regular hectic schedule. She entered therapy at the recommendation of a friend who noticed a disturbing lack of affect, and it became clear quite quickly that she had in fact become an automaton who could do what needed to be done but who was emotionally detached from it all. By repeatedly showing her how widespread her reaction was the therapist was able to help start the work of grieving and of recovery. She was then able not only to perform but also to enjoy.

The task confronting the therapist dealing with complicated grief is to understand the nature of the attachment to the lost pet. It would be useful to the therapist to know what the relationship with the pet meant and how it was influenced by other current or past relationships with others. Individuals struggling to accept the death of a pet are likely to be reliving earlier emotional disappointment, often from their formative years. An appreciation of this historical connection may contribute to an understanding of the depth and scope of the current grief reaction. The task confronting the patient is no less difficult—to come to terms with the fact that present as well as past losses may not be retrieved, and that life has to accommodate disappointments no matter how profound and long lived.

What to Expect (and What Not to Expect) from a Therapist

The particular intervention that a therapist may choose in the case of complicated bereavement will depend on the specifics of the case. Generally, therapists helping the bereaved are most successful when they encourage their clients to recall in great detail what was lost and the circumstances surrounding the loss. A review by the bereaved of actions taken or not taken is an effective way of dealing with existing or potential guilt feelings. In fact a review of the entire relationship, with its highs and its lows, makes it easier to work through the finality of its loss. Additional relevant factors may be other losses that have occurred recently and how they may affect reactions to the present loss, and the existence of reliable support systems that may assist in recovery. The therapist can then point to connections that the client is unaware of, but also utilize resources that already exist. A very distraught young woman who felt very alone following the death of her pet was shocked to discover supportive reactions from her extended family when encouraged by her therapist to contact them and tell them about the animal's death. Instead of hearing, as she expected, "Mary is having a problem again," she heard a genuine expression of sympathy followed by an invitation for dinner, which this time she accepted.

Tempted as s/he may be, a therapist is not going to give advice when it is in the best interest of the person in treatment to reach an independent decision or make an independent choice. An important element in helping the bereaved is providing information as to what might happen next and what options are open. But letting the bereaved choose freely among the options rather than providing advice is critical to avoid dependence and passivity and to encourage efforts to exert control over the environment. Also, the therapist is not likely to take sides with any member of the family when no consensus is reached; rather, issues related to the difficulties in reaching decisions are discussed, and members are assisted in working together toward a resolution that would be acceptable to everybody. A case in point was the R. family which was in severe distress following the death of the family dog, Stan. The veterinarian who referred them described a family whose members yelled at each other even immediately upon learning of Stan's death, and was struck by the absence of any compassion or support. In therapy the same behavior manifested itself, each member insisting on being right and immediately being negated. The therapist was able to avoid being drowned in the chaotic family system, and to make at least some family members aware of how the yelling and arguing prevented any kind of genuine communication and sense of safety. Progress was made when these individuals refused to join in screaming matches, and thus allowed thoughtfulness to replace impulsivity. Though clients may urge the therapist to be a referee or an arbiter of truth it is rarely useful for the therapist to provide such shortcuts or for the client to expect them since they tend to be rather ineffectual in the long run. Lasting solutions to problems must be figured out on an individual or familial basis and then practiced and worked through.

Part of this apparent detachment on the part of the therapist may come across as lack of involvement or as disinterest, but the therapist needs to maintain this stance in order to be effective. By keeping personal feelings in check, as s/he is trained to do, the therapist can stay focused on the grief reaction and on the grieving person, and help look for effective ways to end the crisis. The therapist may tell you that while only a limited number of sessions may be required to deal with the crisis, they should occur in rapid succession (two or three times a week). There is an optimal time for action, and in the case of acute grief the time is as close to the loss as possible when people are much less inhibited and controlled and thus more likely to be candid— essential requirements for effective intervention.

From the Therapist's Perspective

While therapists are trained to relate to their patients' experiences without being judgmental, not all of them can relate to pet loss as "justifying" strong emotional reactions. Some, for one reason or another, view pet loss as a relatively benign life event, and any strong reaction is therefore regarded as indicative of pathology. If it proves too difficult for the therapist to fully appreciate the impact of the loss, he or she may not be the best choice to provide help at that time.

The therapist dealing with the bereaved, possibly more so than with any other population, has to be willing to genuinely enter into a trusting relationship in which the most vulnerable and sensitive expressions of a person can be revealed and discussed. S/he must be willing to tolerate the anger, pain, and frustration that are typical of effective bereavement work. Bodily contact in the form of an arm around the shoulder or even a hug, which many therapists find objectionable in their regular work, may be more acceptable in grief work, though both therapist and client have to feel comfortable with it. In working with grieving individuals the therapist has to convey verbally or nonverbally his or her capacity for empathy and for understanding the extent of the loss. Only when the grieving person believes that such understanding is indeed forthcoming can the full range of feelings and reactions be expressed. Therapists whose presence radiates calm and reassurance are likely to be particularly helpful in grief situations.

Being around grief can trigger strong feelings ranging from anger to compassion, as well as a profound sense of helplessness and impotence. It is therefore important that the therapist dealing with grief on a regular basis has addressed his or her own issues surrounding loss and has reached some resolutions in this regard. After all it is not enough to know what the other person is talking about; one has to be able to offer a perspective that allows the other to move on. The therapist has to be at peace with the realization that s/he cannot help the bereaved retrieve the loss but can nevertheless help with the grief work. Because of the intense psychological demands of working with grieving individuals, therapists often recharge their batteries with peer supervision (discussing their work with other professionals without revealing specific identifying details of their clients), or by belonging to organizations that provide forums for addressing work-related stress. Therapists have to make sure that as their clients emerge from their grief and come to terms with their loss they too are ready to move on and see the sunshine. They need to have the ability to repeatedly rejuvenate in order to be willing to repeatedly descend into another person's loss.

We all must realize that there will always be a twinge of sadness but that recovery is achieved when we can tolerate thinking and talking about the loss, when we don't just pretend but are really ready to move on. We may choose to have other pets or satisfy ourselves with memories, but we must reach a point where sadness is at least balanced by the satisfaction of having known the love of a pet.

References

Anderson, R. K., Hart, B. L., and Hart, L. A., eds. (1984). *The Pet Connection: Its Influence on Our Health and Quality of Life.* Minneapolis: University of Minnesota.

Beck, A., and Katcher, A. (1984). *Between Pets and People: The Importance of Animal Companionship.* New York: Perigee.

Bowlby, J. (1979). *The Making and Breaking of Affectional Bonds.* London: Tavistock.

Corr, C. A. (1993). Coping with dying: lessons that we should and should not learn from the work of Elizabeth Kübler-Ross. *Death Studies* 17(1):69–83.

Cusack, O., and Smith, E. (1984). *Pets and the Elderly: The Therapeutic Bond.* New York: Haworth.

Davis, J. M., and Juhasz, A. M. (1985). The preadolescent/pet bond and psychosocial development. In *Pets and the Family,* ed. M. B. Sussman. New York: Haworth.

Doka, K. J. (1989). *Disenfranchised Grief.* New York: Lexington.

Gannon, D. E. (1994). *The Complete Guide to Dog Law.* New York: Howell.

Goose, G. H., and Barnes, M. J. (1994). Human grief resulting from the death of a pet. *Anthrozoos* 7:103–112.

Harlow, H. A., and Harlow, M. K. (1962). The effect of rearing conditions on behavior. *Bulletin of the Menninger Clinic* 26:213–224.

Hart, L. A., and Mader, B. (1992). Pet loss support hotline: the veterinary students' perspective. *Cal Vet* 46:19–22.

Holcomb, R., Jendro, C., Weber, B., and Nahan, U. (1997). Use of aviary to relieve depression in elderly men. *Anthrozoos* 10:32–36.

Kübler-Ross, E. (1969). *On Death and Dying.* New York: Macmillan.

Levinson, B. M. (1978). Pets and personality development. *Psychological Reports* 42:1031–1038.

Manhawalt, B. A. (1986). *The Ties That Bound: Peasant Families in Medieval England.* New York: Oxford University Press.

Paresky, R. H. (1996). Companion animals and other factors affecting young children's development. *Anthrozoos* 9:159–168.

Parkes, C. M. (1972). *Bereavement: Studies of Grief in Adult Life.* Madison, CT: International Universities Press.

Paulus, E., et al. (1984). Death of pets owned by the elderly: implications for veterinary medical practice. In *Pet Loss and Human Bereavement,* ed. W. J. Kay, H. A. Nieburg, A. H. Kutscher, et al. Ames, IA: Iowa State University.

Quesembery, K., and Hillyer, E., eds. (1994). Exotic pet medicine. *Veterinary Clinics of North America: Small Animals Practice* 24(1). Philadelphia: Saunders.

Robin, M., Bensel, R. W., Quigley, J., and Anderson, R. K. (1984). Abused children and their pets. In *The Pet Connection: Its Influence on Our Health and Quality of Life,* ed. R. K. Anderson, B. L. Hart, and L. A. Hart. Minneapolis: University of Minnesota.

Rogers, J., Hart, L. A., and Boltz, R. P. (1993). The role of pet dogs in casual conversations of elderly adults. *Journal of Social Psychology* 133(3):265–277.

Siegel, J. M. (1990). Stressful life events and use of physician services among the elderly: the moderating role of pet ownership. *Journal of Personality and Social Psychology* 58:1081–1086.

Stern, M. (1996). Psychological elements of attachment to pets and responses to pet loss. *Journal of the American Veterinary Medical Association* 209(10):1707–1711.

Tuan, Y. (1984). *Dominance and Affection: The Making of Pets.* New Haven, CT: Yale University Press.

Related Readings

Barker, S. B., and Barker, R. T. (1988). The human–canine bond: Closer than family ties? *Journal of Mental Health Counseling* 10:46–56.

Bowlby, J. (1980). *Attachment and Loss.* New York: Basic Books.

Cochran, L., and Claspell, E. (1987). *The Meaning of Grief: A Dramaturgical Approach to Understanding Emotion.* New York: Greenwood.

Dietrich, D. R., and Shabad, P. C., eds. (1989). *The Problem of Loss and Mourning.* Madison, CT: International Universities Press.

Fogle, B., and Abrahamson, D. (1989). Pet loss: a survey of the attitudes and feelings of practicing veterinarians. *Anthrozoos* 3:143–150.

Gerwolls, M. K., and Labott, S. M. (1994). Adjustment to death of a companion animal. *Anthrozoos* 7:172–187.

Gewirtz, J. L., and Kurtines, W. M., eds. (1991). *Intersections with Attachment.* Hillsdale, NJ: Lawrence Erlbaum.

Harris, J. M. (1982). A study of client grief responses to death or loss in a companion animal veterinary practice. *California Veterinarian* 36:17–19.

Hart, L. A., Hart, B. L., and Mader, B. (1990). Human euthanasia and companion animal death: caring for the animal, the client, and the veterinarian. *Journal of the American Veterinary Medical Association* 197:1292–1299.

Herzog, H. A., and Burghardt, G. M. (1987). Attitudes toward animals: origins and history. *Anthrozoos* 1:214–222.

Kay, W. J., Cohen, S. P., and Nieburg, H. A., eds. (1988). *Euthanasia of the Companion Animal: The Impact on Pet Owners, Veterinarians, and Society.* Philadelphia: Charles Press.

Kay, W. J., Nieburg, H. A., and Kutscher, A. H., eds. (1984). *Pet Loss and Human Bereavement.* Ames, IA: Iowa State University.

Keddie, K. M. G. (1977). Pathological mourning after the death of a domestic pet. *British Journal of Psychiatry* 131:21–25.

Kidd, A. H., and Kidd, R. M. (1987). Seeking a theory of the human/companion animal bond. *Anthrozoos* 1:140–145.

Kowalski, G. (1991). *The Souls of Animals.* Walpole, NH: Stillpoint.

Kutscher, A. H., and Beck, A. M., eds. (1983). *New Perspective on Our Lives with Companion Animals.* Philadelphia: University of Pennsylvania.

Lagoni, L., Butler, C., and Hetts, S. (1994). *The Human–Animal Bond and Grief.* Philadelphia: Saunders.

Leick, N., and Davidsen-Nielsen, M. (1991). *Healing Pain: Attachment, Loss and Grief Therapy.* New York: Routledge.

Lemieux, C. M. (1988). *Coping with The Loss of a Pet.* Philadelphia: Wallace R. Clarck.

Levinson, B. M. (1965). The veterinarian and mental hygiene. *Mental Hygiene* 49:320–323.

Masson, J., and McCarthy, S. (1995). *When Elephants Weep: The Emotional Lives of Animals.* New York: Dell.

McElroy, S. C. (1996). *Animals as Teachers and Healers.* Sherman Oaks, CA: New Saga.

Nieburg, H. A., and Fisher, A. (1982). *Pet Loss: A Thoughtful Guide for Adults and Children.* New York: Harper & Row.

Parkes, C. M., and Stevenson, J. (1982). *The Place of Attachment in Human Behavior.* New York: Basic Books.

Rando, T. A. (1993). *Treatment of Complicated Mourning.* Champaign, IL: Research Press.

———, ed. (1986). *Loss and Anticipatory Grief.* Lexington, MA: Lexington.

Randolph, M. (1988). *Dog Law.* Berkley, CA: Nolo.

Rydan, H. (1975). *God's Dog*. New York: Coward, McCann.

Rynearson, E. K. (1978). Humans and pets and attachment. *British Journal of Psychiatry* 133:550–555.

Sife, W. (1993). *The Loss of a Pet*. New York: Howell.

Strum, S. (1987). *Almost Human: A Journey into the World of Baboons*. New York: Random House.

Zunin, L. M., and Zunin, H. S. (1991). *The Art of Condolence*. New York: Harper Perennial.

Index

Abuse, of animals, legal issues, 110–112
Accidents, pet loss, 129–131
Acquisition. *See* Pet acquisition
Activity, elderly, advantages of pet ownership to, 58, 63
Age
  aging pets, 94–100
  pet acquisition, 80–82
Aggression, pet ownership, 28–29
American Animal Hospital Association, 62
Anderson, R. K., 59
Animal abuse, legal issues, 110–112
Animal control regulations, legal issues, 107
Animal shelters, lost pets, 129

Animal temperament, family dynamics, pet acquisition and, 79–80
Aristotle, 103
Art, pets and, 23–24
ASPCA, 57
Attachment concept
  needs, 15–20
    companionship, 15–16
    learning source, 18–19
    loss and grief, 19
    reliable partnership, 17–18
    security, 15
    sense of being needed, 16–17
    sense of worth and competence, 17
  overview of, 3–4, 7–10
  principles of, 10–14

Attachment concept (*continued*)
  durability, 11
  early establishment, 13–14
  emotional connection and
    range, 11–13
  specificity, 10–11
  prolonged grief, 184–185

Barnes, M. J., 63
Beck, A., 59
Bereavement. *See* Grief
Birds, pet acquisition, 84
Bowlby, J., 7
Breeders, pet acquisition, 78–79
Breeding, historical perspective
    on, 26–28
Burial, pet loss, 176

Cats
  domestication of, 23
  elderly people, 61
  historical perspective on, 24
  popularity of, 74
Chaucer, G., 145
Children. *See also* Family dynamics
  attachment concept, 13–14
  loss of pet, xvi
  pet loss and, 161–171
    coping strategies, 166–171
    example of, 164–166
    generally, 161–164
  pet ownership and, 9–10, 42–44
  sibling rivalry, 45–46
Cognitive factors, grief, 150–152
Communication
  pet loss, children and, 168–169
  pet ownership and, 44–45

Companionship, attachment
    concept, 15–16
Coping strategies, pet loss,
    children and, 166–171
Corr, C. A., 147
Cremation, pet loss, 176
Cusack, O., 57, 59

Davis, J. M., 44
Death. *See* Life and death issues;
    Pet loss
Delta Society, 59
Disasters, pet loss, 131–133
Dogs
  behavior of, 28–29
  breeding of, 26–28
  domestication of, 23
  popularity of, 74
Doka, K. J., 145
Domestication, of animals, 23
Durability, attachment concept,
    11

Economic factors. *See* Financial
    factors
Egypt (ancient), 24
Elderly, 55–66
  activity expansion, 63
  advantages of pet ownership to,
    57–59
  help for, 60–61
  living arrangements, 59–60
  loss of pet, xvii, 63–66
  mutual supports, 61–62
  overview, 55–57
  pet selection, 61

surviving pets, legal issues,
    112–113
veterinary care, house calls, 62
Emotional factors
    attachment concept, 8. *See also*
        Attachment concept
    elderly, advantages of pet
        ownership to, 57–59
    euthanasia, xvii
    grief, 149. *See also* Grief
Energy considerations, pet
    acquisition, 74–75
Entry restrictions, legal issues, 105
Euthanasia, 137–141
    children and, 169
    emotional factors, xvii
    overview, 137–140
    questions for, 140–141
Exotics, pet acquisition, 84–87

Family dynamics, 41–52. *See also*
        Children
    animal temperament and, pet
        acquisition, 79–80
    euthanasia, 138–139
    overview, 41–47
    pet relationships, 32–33
    sick pets and, 49–50
    vacations, 47–49
    veterinary expenses, 50–52
Federal Emergency Management
    Agency (FEMA), 132–133
Ferrets, pet acquisition, 84–85
Financial factors
    euthanasia, 140
    pet acquisition, 76–77

veterinary expenses, family
    dynamics, 50–52
Fish
    acquisition considerations,
        73–74
    exotic, pet acquisition, 85
Folklore, pets and, 23–24

Gannon, D. E., 104
Gender differences, attachment
    concept, 12
Goose, G. H., 63
Grief, 145–157
    attachment concept, 19
    children, pet loss and, 161–171
    cognitive factors, 150–152
    emotional factors, 149
    experience of, 152–157
    overview, 145–148
    physical reactions, 148–149
    prolonged, 183–198
        described, 183–186
        group supports, 188–191
        personal support, 186–188
        therapist help, 193–198
        veterinarian help, 191–192
    spiritual factors, 150
Group supports, prolonged grief,
    188–191
Guilt, prolonged grief, 184

Harlow, H. A., 8
Harlow, M. K., 8
Hart, L. A., 64
Health benefits, elderly, advan-
    tages of pet ownership to, 59
Hillyer, E., 84

Holcomb, R., 59
Housing regulations, legal issues,
    106
Humane Society, 111–112

Identification, pet loss, protection,
    126
Ill pets. *See* Sick pets
Infant–mother relationship,
    attachment concept, 7–9

Juhasz, A. M., 44

Katcher, A., 59
Kübler-Ross, E., 146, 147

Leases, housing regulations, legal
    issues, 106
Legal issues, 103–113
    animal abuse, 110–112
    animal control regulations, 107
    entry restrictions, 105
    housing regulations, 106
    malpractice laws, 109–110
    overview, 103–104
    property damage, 107–109
    public health, 104
    sanitary controls, 105
    surviving pets, 112–113
    travel regulations, 105–106
Levinson, B. M., 43
Life and death issues. *See also*
    Grief; Pet loss
    elderly, loss of pet, 63–66
    pet relationships, 36–37
Life spans, of pets, 91–94

Lifestyle factors, pet acquisition,
    77–79
Literature
    pet loss, 175–176
    pets and, 23–24
Loss of pet. *See* Pet loss
Lost pets. *See also* Pet loss
    animal shelters, 129
    dealing with, 125
    publicity, 128–129
    telephone, 129

Mader, B., 64
Malpractice laws, legal issues,
    109–110
Manhawalt, B. A., 24
Medical expenses. *See* Veterinary
    expenses
Memorials, pet loss, 175–176
Mortality. *See* Life and death
    issues; Pet loss
Motivation, pet acquisition, 80

Natural disasters, pet loss,
    131–133
Needs, attachment concept,
    15–20. *See also* Attachment
    concept
Neighbors, pet loss, protection,
    127
Nursing homes, pets and, 59–60

Organizations, pet acquisition,
    78–79
Orientation of animal, pet loss,
    protection, 127

Paresky, R. H., 44
Parkes, C. M., 57
Paulus, E., 64
Personality development, pets
    and, 44
Pet acquisition, 73–87
    age, 80–82
    animal temperament and
        family dynamics, 79–80
    energy considerations, 74–75
    exotics, 84–87
    financial factors, 76–77
    lifestyle factors, 77–79
    motivation, 80
    selection of, elderly, 61
    space considerations, 75
    time considerations, 73–74
    veterinary care, 82–84
Pet loss. *See also* Lost pets
    accidents, 129–131
    adjustment to, xviii–xix
    attachment concept, 19
    children and, 161–171
        coping strategies, 166–171
        example of, 164–166
        generally, 161–164
    disasters, 131–133
    elderly, 63–66
    emotional factors, xvi–xviii
    grief, 145–157. *See also* Grief
    memorials, 175–176
    overview, 117–118, 121–125
    protection, 126–128
    replacement pets, 177–180
Pets
    aging of, 94–100

elderly and, 55–66. *See also*
    Elderly
historical perspective on, 23–29,
    103
legal issues, 103–113. *See also*
    Legal issues
life spans of, 91–94
personality development and,
    44
relationships with, xv–xvi,
    29–37
    association with another
        human, 35–36
    centrality of pet, 30–31
    exchanges, 31–32
    family dynamics, 32–33
    life and death issues, 36–37
    overview, 29–30
    power component, 24–27
    projection, 34–35
    self image, 33–34
    shared experience, 31
Photographs, pet loss, protection,
    127–128
Physical reactions, grief, 148–149
Power component, pet–human
    relationship, 24–27
Premise security, pet loss, protec-
    tion, 126–127
Projection, pet relationships,
    34–35
Property damage, legal issues,
    107–109
Protection
    elderly, advantages of pet
        ownership to, 58
    pet loss, 126–128

Public health, legal issues, 104, 105
Publicity, lost pets, 128–129

Quesembery, K., 84

Religion, grief, 150
Replacement pets, pet loss, 177–180
Robin, M., 12
Rogers, J., 57

Safety, elderly, advantages of pet ownership to, 58
Sanitary controls, legal issues, 105
Security
  attachment concept, 15
  pet loss, protection, 126–127
Self image, pet relationships, 33–34
Shelters. *See* Animal shelters
Sibling rivalry, pet ownership and, 45–46
Sick pets, family dynamics and, 49–50
Siegel, J. M., 57
Smith, E., 57, 59
Social factors, elderly, advantages of pet ownership to, 58–59
Space considerations, pet acquisition, 75
Specificity, attachment concept, 10–11
Spiritual factors, grief, 150

Stern, M., 30
Stolen pets, dealing with, 125
Support groups, prolonged grief, 188–191
Surviving pets, legal issues, 112–113

Telephone, lost pets, 129
Temperament, of animal, family dynamics, pet acquisition and, 79–80
Therapist help, prolonged grief, 193–198
Time considerations, pet acquisition, 73–74
Travel regulations, legal issues, 105–106
Tuan, Y., 24

Vacations, family dynamics, 47–49
Veterinary care
  accidents, pet loss, 129–131
  aging pets, 94–100
  elderly, house calls, 62
  life spans of pets, 93–94
  malpractice laws, 109–110
  pet acquisition, 82–84, 86–87
  prolonged grief, 191–192
Veterinary expenses
  elderly and, 65
  family dynamics, 50–52
  pet acquisition and, 77

Zodiac, 25
Zoos, 27

About the Authors

Michael Stern, Ph.D., is a clinical psychologist practicing in both New York and New Jersey. He is an adjunct associate professor at Teachers' College of Columbia University, a supervisor at Yeshiva University and at The Institute for Contemporary Psychotherapy, and a consultant to the New York City Police Department. Dr. Stern is a graduate of the New York University Postdoctoral Program and the president of its Psychoanalytic Society. He lives in New Jersey with his family and various pets.

Susan Cropper, D.V.M., received her doctorate from Kansas State University in 1964 as one of only three women in her graduating class. In 1975, following eleven years of relatively traditional office and farm practice in both Indiana and New Jersey, she chose to establish her house call veterinary practice. After thirty-three years in full time practice, Dr. Cropper still finds her work (and her patients, and clients) as fulfilling, rewarding, and absolute fun as on the first day.